The Myth of the Paperless Office

The Myth of the Paperless Office

Abigail J. Sellen and Richard H. R. Harper

The MIT Press
Cambridge, Massachusetts
London, England

First MIT Press paperback edition, 2003
© 2002 Massachusetts Institute of Technology

This book was set in Sabon by Achorn Graphic Services, Inc.
Printed and bound in the United States of America.

Library of Congress Cataloging-in-Publication Data

Sellen, Abigail J.
  The myth of the paperless office / Abigail J. Sellen and Richard H. R. Harper.
    p. cm.
  Includes bibliographical references and index.
  ISBN 0-262-19464-3 (hc. : alk. paper), 0-262-69283-X (pb)
  1. Office equipment and supplies. 2. Paper. I. Harper, Richard (Richard H. R.)
  II. Title.

HF5521 .S43   2001
651.5—dc21

                                                              2001032626

10 9 8 7 6 5 4

For Christina, Harry, Stan, Ann, and John

Contents

Acknowledgments

As with most research, there are many individuals who contribute but never see their name on the final product. Given that this work has been undertaken over a number of years and in different research establishments, there are many such people to thank.

The institution that played the largest part in this work was Xerox's research lab in Cambridge, England. It was here where we first met and commenced the research; but it was here also where we met various other individuals who deserve a special thank you. Our erstwhile colleagues Marge Eldridge, Kenton O'Hara, and William Newman all played major roles not only as active researchers in various studies of paper but also as friends and advisers. Kenton, in particular, led most of the research on reading reported in chapter 4, and we are indebted to him for his work and insights. There were also many other people in the lab, at Xerox PARC in California, and elsewhere in the corporation, who influenced our thinking and provided the forum to develop our ideas. They include Bob Anderson (director of the lab in Cambridge), research colleagues Graham Button, Mik Lamming, and Allan Maclean, as well as support staff Michelle Heydon, Christine King, and Mike Molloy. Outside of Xerox's research labs, we are grateful to David Jones, who helped set up the research in the first place; Ted Carroll, who helped undertake it; Paul Ratcliffe, who encouraged us to present it to the corporation; and Gene Golovchinsky, of Fuji Xerox, who has advised us on a variety of matters regarding e-books.

Moving on to Hewlett-Packard Labs, Bristol, many other colleagues helped see the book through to completion. Draft chapters have greatly benefited from input from Barry Brown, David Frohlich, Erik Geelhoed, Alison Kidd, and Simon Lewis. The book would also never have been finished had it not been for management's lending moral support and making it possible to balance work on the book with HP's more immediate concerns. Here thanks go to Janet Bruten, Colin I'Anson, and Martin Merry. Finally, we are also grateful to Lin Jones for making life easier and David Ball, of HP Labs Information Centre, for help in tracking down information at short notice.

At the Digital World Research Centre, University of Surrey, we thank Lynne Hamill, Neville Moray, and Alex Taylor for their help and forbearance. Thanks also to many other colleagues whose concerns may sometimes have been sidelined because the book has taken precedence. Nonetheless, the auspices of the Centre enabled us to continue our research into paper, and Brian Shatwell, of Future Technology Research at the Post Office, in particular, needs thanking for this.

Outside of the institutions we have worked for, there have been numerous individuals who have advised us as well as influenced us in many ways. We can point here in particular to Bill Buxton, Bill Gaver, Christian Heath, Paul Luff, Don Norman, Dave Randall, and Mark Rouncefield. Don has been especially helpful, advising in ways too numerous to mention. John Senders, of the University of Toronto, has been a lifelong influence on our work. This has been all the more valuable since he was one of the earliest pioneers of the paperless journal.

We have also benefited from many other experts over the years: David Duthie, of the University of Leeds; Nick Wiseman, of the Department of Paper Science, UMIST; and Joe Wright, president of Paprican (the Pulp and Paper Research Institute of Canada).

There is another set of individuals, much larger in number, who contributed to the research in quite a different way: as its subjects. Some we can name, including Christa Dubb, Terry Hill, Warren Minami, and Chris Yandle, of the IMF; and Val Prince and the late Barry Sanderson, of Lancashire Constabulary. However, many must remain anonymous, including the staff of Dantech, UKCom, and the chocolate manufacturing company, as well as air traffic controllers in the United Kingdom and California.

Thanks are also due to those who helped in the preparation of the manuscript. They include Rachel Murphy, for drawing the document life cycle diagrams, and Wendy Mackay, for the pictures of flight strips. Many administrative staff have helped us, including Karin Mitchell and Carol Harris-Lees at the Digital World. Also, staff at MIT Press deserve much thanks both for editorial guidance and encouragement.

Finally, there is our family. We thank our parents for endless childminding and many other unpaid jobs; and we thank our kids, one of whom had the good sense to delay his birth until three days after completion of this manuscript. Though they have little or no interest in the role of paper, except as something to scribble on or use for making airplanes, they certainly know how much time Mum and Dad spent on "the book."

Newbury, England

The Myth of the Paperless Office

1
Introduction

As we write this book, we have paper all around us. On the desk are stacks of articles, rough notes, outlines, and printed e-mail messages. On the wall are calendars, Post-it notes, and photographs. On the shelves are journals, books, and magazines. The filing cabinets and the wastebasket are also full of paper. Among all this sit our computers, on which the composition takes place. Yet, if the computer is the canvas on which documents are created, the top of the desk is the palette on which bits of paper are spread in preparation for the job of writing. Without these bits of paper ready to hand, it is as if the writing, and more especially the *thinking,* could not take place in earnest.

On reflection, there are many other ways that paper is important in the process of producing this book. There is the collaborative process: when one of us finishes some work on a chapter, we print it out and hand it to the other. We read it, mark it up, and then discuss it by flipping through the marked-up pages together. There is the proofreading process: we print out the final version of each chapter to catch the surface-level errors (typos, spelling, and grammar) and, more important, to get a sense of the text and the way it flows. Finally, there is the importance of paper as a tangible object. Ultimately, we want a bound volume in hand—a physical product that testifies to our efforts and that we can hand to family, friends, and colleagues.

But we need not reflect only on our own experiences of producing this book. One has only to look at any workplace to see how firmly paper is woven into the fabric of our lives. Our own workplaces are no exception. In some ways this is ironic. We work in two high-tech research laboratories—one academic and one corporate. As such, we are exposed to more of the latest technological gadgets than most people. We have access to different kinds of computers (desktop, portable, mobile), most with fully networked capabilities. We have the latest software packages for writing, drawing, viewing, and browsing. We have scanners, digital cameras, audio recorders, and video cameras to provide all kinds of interesting input for our digital documents. So why, when we have all the latest technology to allow us to work in the digital world, do we depend on paper so heavily? Indeed, why are most workplaces so dependent on paper? It seems that the promised "paperless office" is as much a mythical ideal today as it was thirty years ago.

As one might expect, the answers to these questions are complex and multifaceted. This book is our attempt to provide some answers as a result of years of studying how and why people use paper in the workplace. Many research reports and analyses over the years have looked at trends in paper consumption and the factors that affect it (technological developments, population demographics, the environment, and so on). When we looked at these analyses, we found ourselves constantly asking, Why? We didn't so much want to see the numbers as to understand where they came from. Why are people still using paper when new technologies have become so readily available? What can we say about paper use in different kinds of workplaces? Are there any lessons to be learned about choosing or designing new technologies from looking at paper use? Where will paper be in the workplace ten or twenty years from now? These are the kinds of questions that really interested us and for which we could find few answers. This led to our studies of office life, and these findings make up the bulk of this book.

Origins of the Myth of the Paperless Office

Let's first take a historical look at the origins of the concept of the paperless office—the expectation that electronic technologies would make paper in the office a thing of the past. As it turns out, it is quite difficult to track down just where and when the term entered common parlance. When we both worked for Xerox, the understanding was that it came from Xerox PARC—Xerox's research lab in Palo Alto, California, the birthplace of many radical ideas that affected the world of technology, including the laser printer, the desktop graphical user interface, and the Ethernet, the technology that connected it all. Pinning down details was difficult, however. In the mid-1970s, when PARC was new, a *Business Week* article featured the then head of PARC, George Pake, making a series of predictions about the office of the future.[1] This article implies as much about the demise of the typewriter as it does about paper. In terms of specific projects at PARC around that time, we heard one story about how there had been a "one-ream office" project, which involved seeking out a guinea pig to see what would happen if someone were limited to keeping and using no more than one ream of paper in his office. Apparently, no one had volunteered. We were later told by others who were at PARC at that time that paperlessness was not an issue for most of the researchers anyway and that it was only "outsiders" who made the claim that that was what PARC was about.

Whatever the truth of the matter, it became clear that PARC researchers had had to steer a careful path in their activities. Paperlessness as a goal ran completely counter to what was then Xerox's main business: the making of money from paper, in particular the copying of one paper document onto another. As it happens, paper is still the main source of Xerox's revenue stream, although the company has now moved into the digital printing marketplace as well. Given this, though the PARC researchers might have had the paperless office in mind, they were not in the right organization to make their views too public.

In any event, long before this, inventors were dreaming up new technologies that aimed to replace the old, paper-based ways of doing things. Here we can go right back to the early 1800s. It was around this time that the roots of electronic mail were born, when Samuel Morse first came up with the idea of transmitting data instantaneously using electricity. By the end of that century, the telegraph, the teletype machine, and the telephone had all appeared. But some inventions were seen as more direct possibilities for replacing paper-based communications. In his book *The Invisible Computer*, Don Norman describes the prospects that opened when Thomas Edison invented the record (or phonograph).[2] The device consisted of a cylinder covered with a thin layer of foil that could "record" the voice of a speaker using the oscillations created by sound to emboss the foil layer as the cylinder turned around. The cylinder could then be "replayed" and the sound reproduced. Doubtless, these terms were a little confusing to the general public completely unfamiliar with the idea of recording or replaying anything, let alone someone's voice. Still, Edison suggested that one of the things that could be done was that managers, instead of dictating to secretaries, could dictate to the device. The cylinder with their words embossed on it could then be sent to colleagues, who would play back the message. They, in turn, could reply by recording their own voices over the first recording. In this way, Edison suggested, there would no longer be paper messages and letters (nor, one might add, a need for secretaries). Hence, this would mark the beginnings of a paperless office.

Decades later, other visionaries were predicting devices that would not just replace paper-based communications but would obviate the use of paper for more extensive document printing and storage. In 1945, Vannevar Bush wrote,

Consider a future device for individual use, which is a sort of mechanized, private file and library. It needs a name, and, to coin one at random, "memex" will do. A memex is a device in which an individual stores his books, records, and communications, and which is mechanized so that it may be consulted with exceeding speed and flexibility. It is an enlarged intimate supplement to his memory.

It consists of a desk, and while it can be presumably operated from a distance, it is primarily the piece of furniture at which he works. On the top are slanting translucent screens, on which material can be projected for convenient reading. There is a keyboard, and sets of buttons and levers. Otherwise it looks like an ordinary desk.[3]

Bush went on to explain how the material would be stored, mainly in the form of microfilm, and how new material would be composed using a system of cameras and film. Here, then, were the beginnings of an idea of an alternative way to search and archive documents.

The advent of computers changed these notions substantially, moving away from microfilm and instead dealing with documents made up of bits and bytes. In the 1950s and 1960s, Bush's original concept began to look more like a prediction of today's digital books and digital libraries. In *Libraries of the Future,* Joseph Licklider wrote, "We need to substitute for the book a device that will make it easy to transmit information without transporting material, and that will not only present information to people but also process it for them, following procedures they specify, apply, monitor, and, if necessary, revise and reapply."[4] Licklider hypothesized a computer-based system with pen input and speech recognition that would help users query vast repositories of information. Both Bush and Licklider were foreseeing the explosion of information to come, recognizing that paper-based systems were simply no longer going to provide adequate solutions for dealing with it.

It is important to note that these pictures of the future were spurred on by excitement about the possibilities of new technologies. Edison and others weren't necessarily all that interested in the fate of paper, being more concerned to illustrate what new things their ideas and inventions might allow people to do. The abandonment of paper was a side effect rather than the key to what the technology made possible. But throughout such writings, paper has always been a symbol of old-fashioned practices and old-fashioned technology. New technologies, as long ago as the mid-1800s, were offering something "better." What we see here is that, again and again, this kind of juxtaposition of paper and new technologies—the one being held up as a poor alternative to the other—was a driving force toward the ideal of the paperless office.

Building on the Myth: The Past Thirty Years

It is therefore not so surprising that although PARC researchers might not have thought they were in the business of inventing the paperless office, others did—particularly journalists who wanted to field a "big story" about the revolution that was about to occur. In the early to mid-1970s, it hardly needed a leap of imagination for the media to perpetuate this idea. When PARC transformed computers from massive and difficult-to-use devices barely removed from Babbage's original conception into machines that could be used on the desktop, it seemed obvious to many that the end of paper was in sight. After all, the Xerox Star system seemed designed to replicate aspects of paper use. The Star had a landscape-oriented screen capable of displaying two portrait pages side by side and was linked via Ethernet to computers with the same configuration. What else was this connection for but to send and receive documents? And what else was the desktop computer for but to compose these documents, storing them in what came to be the first virtual representations of "folders" and "file cabinets"? Not only word-processing applications but also the beginnings of electronic mail were fueling the collective imagination of the press. The future of the electronic office seemed assured, the hegemony of paper doomed.

Yet, for a host of reasons, the revolution in office life that seemed imminent did not occur. For one thing, the costs of the networked systems Xerox initially offered were simply too great for all but the most affluent organizations. Besides, senior staff at Xerox judged that there was no future for such products, irrespective of the price. As is now well known, they "fumbled the future" by withdrawing the systems—only to attempt to bring them back when someone else had produced something similar.[5]

In any event, while they were making up their minds, the path of technological development at PARC became fragmented. One camp wanted to pursue the networked vision, another to develop freestanding desktop applications and word processing (this eventually laid the groundwork for personal computing as we know it). Eventually, the research group at PARC split, with some staying to continue developing the ill-fated Star system and others leaving to join a new division. Meanwhile, a third group from outside of Xerox simply took some of the basic ideas and implemented them on their own, efforts that came to be known first as the Apple Lisa and later as the Apple Macintosh computer.

The end result was that the "information architecture" that PARC had invented, an architecture that was intended to allow seamless connection between users over a network, was implemented only in a limited way outside the laboratory (in the product division that developed the Star system). Perhaps most important, those word-processing applications that successfully made it to the outside world and that seemed nearest to providing an alternative to paper came to be supported mainly by freestanding machines unconnected to one another.

This had an important consequence: paper became in effect the connection between the users of the freestanding machines. By this time, the early 1980s, there was a variety of personal computers on the market (IBM and Apple were already dominant), and the programs for one kind of PC could not be understood by PCs of other kinds. In other words, with notable exceptions (one thinks here of the Xerox Daybreak networked systems, for example), paper became a surrogate for a network, enabling users with different machines to share documents or other materials they were working on.

Though this is rather to oversimplify the matters in question, it gives an idea of the kinds of problems people encountered when they tried to move toward the paperless office: the technology didn't quite offer all the things that they would need. Now, if the attempt we have just described to invent an information architecture at PARC in the 1970s was one period when the paperless office was thought to be near at hand, the early 1990s was another. Between then and the 1970s, the development of technologies had maintained its pace. Indeed, technology had transformed office life. Investments in Apple computers, IBM PCs, and thereafter various clones led many to think that paper would at last disappear because one of the most important jobs it was doing—connecting people—was finding support in a new technology: the Internet, more particularly the World Wide Web. Central to the Web was a fairly simple markup language called HTML, which enabled almost any desktop computer linked to the telephone network to read and display any other computer's documents. In effect, HTML allowed users to bypass the intransigent problem of interoperability between different word-processing and graphics applications. Whereas before the WordPerfect format could not be read by Microsoft Word and vice versa, now with HTML most document applications could be configured to read any other.

This is to simplify a change that involved a host of important and at times complex interdependencies. The provision of low-cost access to the Internet did much to ensure that the benefits of HTML could show themselves, for example. The willingness of computer software companies to develop their applications to read HTML was another. But the end result was that at last people in organizations could begin to effectively communicate with one another. Not only could they send electronic documents to others within their own organizations, whatever machine or system they were using, but they could do the same with people outside their organizational "firewalls." Moreover, they could create new and easily accessed repositories of electronic documents via their intranets. At last the disappearance of paper seemed assured. Anecdotes about the emergence of completely paperless companies spread like wildfire in the business press and even in government pronouncements. Complete transformations in office life were again foretold.

However, renewed hopes that the paperless office would at last appear were to be dashed again. Paper consumption kept rising; the World Wide Web, far from decreasing paper consumption, served to increase the amount of printing done at home and in the office. With the Web, people could access more information more easily than before, but though they used digital means to find and retrieve information, they still preferred to print it out on paper when they wanted to read it.

Now, at the turn of the millennium, further technology developments are renewing predictions of the paperless office, this time developments that seem as if they will radically affect the preference to read on paper. What has spurred this new wave of hope is the fact that technologies are beginning to look and feel more paperlike. Until the mid-1990s, limits on battery power combined with large, heavy screen technologies meant that alternatives to paper for reading of books, memos, and reports were not sufficiently lightweight or portable. But now all that has changed. Both display and battery technologies are thinner and lighter. Devices make use of a variety of wireless protocols, so they no longer need to be tethered to talk to each other or to talk to a server. Pen-based input is also gaining momentum (especially as the major input method for palm-top devices) after some shaky starts in the 1980s. All these aspects are now leading to more portable, mobile devices on which documents can not only be accessed, sent, and read but marked up in a paperlike way. And even more radical technologies are in the offing. Although they have yet to see the light of day outside the laboratory, new ultra-thin display media with a look and feel akin to a sheet of acetate for an overhead projector are being dubbed "electric paper" or "re-imageable paper." Essentially this invention sandwiches a layer of tiny dichromatic balls (black on one side and white on the other) between two plastic sheets. These balls rotate when an electric charge is passed over them. These lightweight sheets can potentially display dynamic data and be stacked, hung on walls, and even rolled up almost like paper.

Again we hear media pronouncements about the end of paper, the death of the book, and so on. This time, it is claimed, these new technologies lead not only to the paperless office but also to the paperless home.

The Reality

State of the Paper Industry

All this prompts one to ask, What is the state of the paper industry at the start of the twenty-first century? Given all the expectations of the media and the public, it is perhaps not surprising that the relative stock valuation of paper companies compared to the world index is now much lower than it was a few years ago. Investors do not believe that the future is in paper stocks. Of course, one might think this is merely a function of the "dot.com" fascination that has, until very recently, created distortion in the marketplace. But as figure 1.1 shows, the diminishing value of paper stocks (relatively speaking) has been a trend going back several years.

Figure 1.1
The value of forest products and paper stocks as against a world index of stocks, 1993–2000 (Stock Watch International). Note: See *Pulp & Paper International* (June, 2000), p. 13.

Despite this, the actual output of the paper industry is greater than ever. Recent data show that over the course of the year 1999 global paper and board output increased by 4.6 percent, to a total 316 million tons. The top producer was North America, with an output of 108 million tons in 1999, followed by Europe (94 million tons) and Asia (92 million tons).[6]

Such significant increases have been typical in the last couple of decades. According to the American Forest and Paper Association, U.S. paper shipments of all types increased by 40 percent in the thirteen years from 1980 to 1993.[7] Similar growth was seen in the United Kingdom for paper and board consumption between 1986 and 1996 (increasing from 8.7 to 11.5 million tonnes).[8] More recent data show that although there is considerable regional variation across the globe, consumption has for the most part been substantial over the last ten years (figure 1.2).

These overall figures may not necessarily be all that significant. First, they reflect all kinds of paper consumption, including paper for packaging and sanitary materials. Second, paper demand is subject to a wide range of factors, including changes in general economic conditions, employment trends, and population demographics. But, as it turns out, evidence for paper consumption in the office tells a similar story.

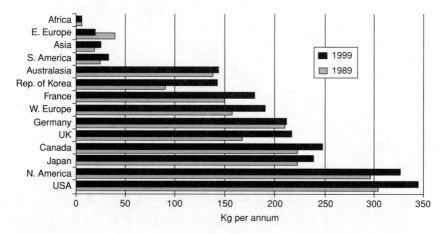

Figure 1.2
Per capita consumption of paper and board by region, 1989 and 1999 (Paper Federation of Great Britain). (*Source:* Reprinted with permission from the Web site of The Paper Federation of Great Britain (Nov., 2000) at <http://www.paper.org.uk/htdocs/Statistics/capita.html>.)

Table 1.1
Office Paper Consumption in the United States by Paper Grade, 1995 and 2000

Paper Grade	1995 Tons (000)	2000 Tons (000)	Percent Growth
Uncoated free-sheet	13,654.42	15,669.09	14.7
Coated free-sheet	4,357.16	5,288.27	21.3
Uncoated groundwood	4,959.77	4,635.69	−6.5
Bristols	1,378.70	1,705.75	23.7

Source: The Future of Paper: Executive Summary, CAP Ventures Report, (Norwell: MA 1995), p. 22. Available from Communication Supplies Consulting Service, CAP Ventures Inc.

Office paper use constitutes 30–40 percent of total paper consumption (at least in the United States and the United Kingdom).[9] This includes not only ordinary cut-sheet office paper for printing but also paper for business communications and business-related publishing products such as technical manuals, professional reference books, and directories. Growth estimates in office paper consumption in the United States in 1995 and 2000 are shown in table 1.1. There are some technical terms here that need explaining.

Four paper grades are used in office environments, the first being *uncoated free-sheet.* Uncoated free-sheet makes up the largest proportion of the paper used in offices, for everything from general printing to personal printing. *Coated free-sheet* is used for more expensive advertising materials. *Uncoated groundwood* is used heavily for forms and other transactional documents, and *Bristols* are used for books, reference manuals, and so on. Aside from the reduction in the specialist market for uncoated groundwood,[10] which is a very small proportion of the total market, these figures indicate substantial growth in office paper consumption.

If we look at the data over a longer time span, we see that office paper consumption (paper for all printing and writing, that is, all paper excluding newsprint, packaging, tissues, and specialty grades) has increased steadily and linearly over the past twenty years or so in Europe, North America, and the world (figure 1.3). The bottom line is that no slowdown in office paper consumption appears on the horizon. In fact, if we look at

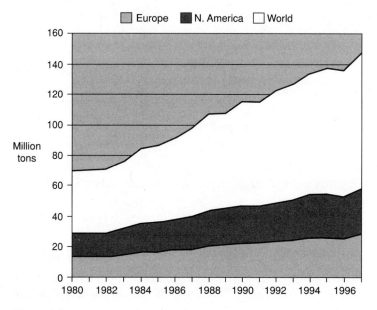

Figure 1.3
Office paper consumption in Europe, the United States, and the world, 1980–1997 (*Pulp & Paper International,* July issues 1981–1998).

the figures for worldwide consumption, the trend is a steady, steep increase.

Changes in Office Technology and Paper Use

The basic message from looking at paper industry trends is that the new technologies we have discussed, from the personal computer to the Internet to portable pen-based computing, have so far failed to have the predicted effect on paper consumption. We have also seen this for ourselves. Many of the workplaces we have studied have tried to go paperless, paying consultants to recommend the best digital solutions, organizing task forces to assess company needs, and buying and implementing the most up-to-date systems available. We have seen varying success in reducing paper use, ranging from dismal failure to mild reduction. We have also seen varying success in altering an organization's work practices, from complete rejection of new systems to major overhauls of the ways of working. We have heard stories of paperless offices, but we have never seen one. More commonly, the introduction of new technology does not get rid of paper; it either increases it or shifts the ways in which it is used. For example, in one organization, managers banned the use of personal filing cabinets, only to find that people resorted to using their cars or home offices to store their paper files.

What can we attribute this to? Why is this happening? To be sure, there have been remarkable changes in technology development in the past three decades. However, it is clear that some of these developments have fed people's inclination to print. There are two significant technological trends we can point to here.

Trend 1 The first trend is that advances in interconnectivity mean that we have access to much more information than before. More and more workplaces are now fully networked; more and more people are linked up to the Internet, not only in the workplace but also in the home. Recent claims are that Internet traffic doubles about every nine months.

This, coupled with cheaper connectivity and increases in network bandwidth, means that people can bring more information to their desktops (at work or at home), are more likely to be connected with other people, and have the ability to quickly and easily send information to one another. One might suppose that this would result in decreased reliance on paper, but quite the opposite appears to be the case.

In a survey of 150 companies in the United States, information technology (IT) managers reported that introducing networked access to the Internet and to the company intranet caused a noticeable increase in the amount of printing in their organizations from desktop and work group printers.[11] It seems that much of the information found on the Web needs to be printed in order for us to read it and make sense of it. Another more recent study found that the introduction of e-mail into an organization caused, on average, a 40 percent increase in paper consumption.[12] While the use of e-mail for sending and distributing documents, messages, and memos has reduced the role of paper for the delivery itself, it has not done away with paper altogether. Many e-mail messages and e-mailed attachments (especially the longer ones) tend to get printed. The availability of e-mail also means that people get more messages than they ever received when they used paper mail. It seems that the more information people receive and have access to, the more people need to print it.

Trend 2   A second major trend is the advancement of print technology itself. In the past twenty years or so, there have been quite substantial changes in the ways documents get printed and what they consist of. Previously, if you wanted to distribute copies of a document to your colleagues, you printed it out first, photocopied it, and then distributed it. Today, rather than print and distribute, we distribute and then print. In other words, we send the file electronically to the recipient, who then prints it out. This is underlined by the fact that between 1988 and 1993, the worldwide installed base of copiers increased by only 5 percent, whereas the worldwide installed base of printers increased by 600 percent.[13] In other words, more than ten years ago, paper-to-paper production was being supplanted by electronic-to-paper production at an extremely rapid rate. Copying is now giving way to what is called in the business MOPying, or the process of producing Multiple-Original single Prints. Prints are now more likely to originate directly from a digital source. With the newest copying techniques, even when a user makes a copy of a paper document, that document is scanned first, converted to a digital file, and then printed.

Printing is now not only digital but on-demand. Whereas before, production printing was often done through large commercial offset printers who would produce predefined print runs, new networked digital printers allow people to have documents printed as and when they need them. More and more large organizations have been making the conversion to digital on-demand printing. For example, in the United States these include major document consumers such as Boeing, the U.S. Navy, the Patent and Trademark Office, and the Internal Revenue Service. Large corporations are not the only ones who are changing. There are many changes, too, in the way work group and personal printing gets done. Improved publishing software, e-services, and printing architectures let people design what they want and print only what they need.

A final factor with regard to printing is that printers are now cheaper, faster, and of better quality than before. Color printing is now commonplace, and it is likely that the black-and-white printer will soon go the way of the black-and-white TV. People and organizations have more control over what they print, when they print, and because of networking, where they print. We are all becoming our own publishers, editors, printers, and distributors.

Thus, in the last decade, new technologies have provided the means by which we can produce low-cost, high-quality, personalized paper documents. It is no surprise, then, that we are all taking advantage of this and are consuming more paper than ever.

However, if new technologies are encouraging our use of paper, they also enable us to work more effectively with digital documents. For example:

• Word-processing applications in the Western world have virtually replaced the typewriter for the creation, modification, and reuse of work-related and personal documents, memos, and mail.

• E-mail is commonplace and has practically eradicated the paper inter office memo in modern workplaces. Electronic delivery is now the main way for sending and distributing documents, messages, and memos within and between organizations.

• Computers are smaller, more lightweight, and wireless with longer-lasting batteries. Working with digital documents and accessing networks while on the move is easier than ever.

• Many paper directories, reference manuals, dictionaries, encyclopedias, technical documentation, forms, catalogues, newsletters, magazines, and journals are being made available in electronic form on CD-ROMs or online.

• There are more online, networked databases and search tools for publishing, finding, and retrieving information. Internet-based applications such as the World Wide Web have been replacing other kinds of digital databases as well as paper-based document stores.

• Increasingly, paper-based interorganizational documentation for contracts and other transactional activities is being replaced with electronic business transactions and electronic data interchange (EDI) for automatic digital business transactions. (This is the main reason for the decreased use of uncoated groundwood, the preferred paper for such documents.)

• Cheaper, better scanning and imaging devices, and software for conversion of paper documents into digital form, have made digital archiving of legacy paper documents easier.

• Cheaper, more efficient digital archiving media are making possible the storage of vast amounts of digital information. This includes CD-ROM and magneto-optical storage, magnetic tape subsystems, digital video-discs, and networked hard drives and disk arrays. In 1995, it was estimated that 95 percent of all documents in organizations were stored on paper with the remaining 5 percent stored digitally.[14] The proportion of paper-stored documents is thought to have decreased substantially in the last few years.

Putting all this evidence together makes it rather difficult to understand what effect the introduction of digital technologies is having overall. Some years ago, Paul Saffo likened the situation to an electronic piñata[15] surrounded by a thin layer of paper. As the electronic core grows, so too does the surface of the sphere, though at a much slower rate. In hindsight, Saffo's view seems to have been correct: the volume of paper-based information has continued to grow more or less linearly, while the volume of electronic information has increased exponentially.

The "Affordances" of Paper

So, the relation between digital technologies and paper in office life is much more complex than one might think. Often, it seems that the new technologies shift the point at which paper is used rather than replacing its use altogether. We see this in the shift from photocopying to digital printing and how the point at which the printing takes place is altered (previously before distribution; now after it). In either case, paper is still consumed. We have also seen that new technologies can radically alter office work: sometimes the digital technologies do away with the need for paper, but other times they create more demand for it.

To understand why this is so, we need a better grasp of the reasons that paper supports some kinds of human activities better than the digital alternatives do. We need to understand what it is about the physical properties of paper that make it play into different aspects of the work that people do, and how work practices have evolved along with paper in such a way that paper is woven into the very fabric of work. It is only by looking carefully at people's interactions with paper artifacts, and with the digital technologies they have to hand, that we can hope to predict the circumstances under which they might be willing to give paper up. To some extent, this will be a matter of providing people with better technological alternatives, but it also means being sensitive to their existing work practices so that we can know what their requirements might be and how change can be introduced.

To take this view is to see paper not as a *problem* in organizational life but as *a way of looking* at organizational life. In other words, it is to view paper as a way of understanding the work that people do and the reasons they do it that way. Later, in chapter 6, we show how understanding paper use can be a resource for change. It can help determine which existing digital technologies might support people's work and how digital devices might be better designed to do this.

To help us understand paper use, we employ a concept called "affordances." The notion of affordances can be traced back to the ecological psychologist J. J. Gibson in his seminal book *The Ecological Approach to Visual Perception*. Gibson's theory was that people "pick up" information about their environment and the objects in it largely by attending to what those objects *afford*. An affordance refers to the fact that the physical properties of an object make possible different functions for the person perceiving or using that object. In other words, the properties of objects determine the possibilities for action. Consider what Gibson said about tools:

An elongated object, especially if weighted at one end and graspable at the other, affords hitting or hammering (a club). A graspable object with a rigid sharp edge affords cutting and scraping (a knife, a hand axe, or a chopper). A pointed object affords piercing (a spear, an arrow, an awl, or a needle). These tools may be combined in various ways to make other tools.[16]

The physical properties of paper (its being thin, light, porous, opaque, flexible, and so on) afford many different human actions, such as grasping, carrying, manipulating, folding, and in combination with a marking tool, writing on. These affordances of paper, then, are about what people can do with paper. If paper is used to make different kinds of objects, those objects take on a different set of affordances. For example, bind the pieces of paper together into a book, and it affords flicking through and reading from. Its fixed arrangement of pages affords placeholding and knowing where you are within the book.

Digital technologies, too, have affordances. A desktop PC, for example, is not light, thin, and flexible, so it does not afford carrying (very easily), folding, grasping, and so on. But because it dynamically displays information, it affords the viewing of moving images. Because it has a keyboard, it affords the creation of regular, geometric, uniform marks. Because it makes use of digital storage, it affords the storing and accessing of large amounts of information. Digital technologies, however, tend to present much more complicated interfaces to their users than most of the physical objects we encounter in everyday life. Acting on and interpreting feedback from our actions with devices such as desktop computers often require a great deal of learning and experience. Don Norman has argued in various books,[17] that this is because many of the affordances of digital devices are hidden from view. Many of their features cannot be perceived and thus are never used.

By employing this notion of affordance, we can begin to concentrate on what paper, as a physical artifact, makes possible for the people who use it and for the kind of work they do. It allows us to ask what actions are possible and what goals are achievable when people use paper, or what they *cannot* do or achieve when they use paper. The physical properties of paper make many actions not possible and many activities not achievable. We can then compare and contrast these affordances of paper with those of existing digital devices. More interesting, we can begin to think about what new kinds of devices or systems might be constructed that would make new kinds of activities possible or better support the kinds of work that people are trying to accomplish. All this, then, helps us to reason about what kinds of changes will be necessary before people will favor new technologies over their old tools and artifacts.

The notion of affordance has therefore been pivotal to our research and is a central theme of this book. It is a concept that has enabled us to focus on the nature of people's interaction with the tools and resources that they have at hand in the work they do. The nature of this interaction is often bound up with people's work practices and even with social and cultural factors in organizations.

Overview of the Book

Our task in this book, then, is to show how this approach to paper use has yielded new insights into understanding work, documents, and the use of new technologies. It is also to show how this approach can help in the design process. Finally, it is to show how this deeper understanding can enable predictions about the role of paper as we move further into the digital age. This is, or should be, a serious concern for organizations that develop new technologies or that rely heavily on paper for their revenue. But it is also a concern for organizations that wish to keep abreast of the latest technological trends in order to exploit them in their business processes. As most organizations realize, new technologies need considerable forethought before being introduced into working life. New ways of working need to take the old ways into account. Central to these old ways is the role of paper. If organizations can understand where paper is useful and, more important, why it is useful, they may be able to make better-informed judgments about how new and old technologies will work together.

To this end, this book is about what we have been finding out about paper over the last several years. As far as we know, ours has been the only program of research aimed at examining paper from the point of view of *why* and *how* it is used. There have been trend analyses of paper use and some case studies that point toward the issues, but we have undertaken (with the valuable help of colleagues[18]) a series of studies of people using paper both in real work settings and in more controlled laboratory settings. To do this we have made use of whatever methods seemed best to help us find answers. We have used observations and interviews, asked people to keep diaries, videotaped them, and studied the documents they use. We have drawn liberally from standard methods in our own disciplines (sociological ethnography and cognitive psychology) as well as invented new methods when it seemed appropriate. Because of this, we have been able to look at paper use at many different levels, from the dynamics of people's behavior with paper at a local level up to the level of organizational culture and practice.

We explore in chapter 2 why paper is usually seen as a problem in organizational life. We find that paper can be a problem on different levels. First, there is the *symbolic problem.* Here we elaborate on the notion that

paper is often thought of as a symbol of the old-fashioned past and a failure to progress to a modern, high-tech world. One of the concerns for any
investigation into paper is to separate this symbolic aspect from real and
quantifiable concerns. These concerns are our second topic, which we call
the *cost problem*. We compare the real costs of paper versus digital systems
in terms of time, effort, and resources. Finally, we discuss the *interactional
problem*. This has to do with the limitations of paper as a tool and a technology at point of use. For example, we discuss how it supports only local
use, how it is difficult to reuse or modify, and how it is costly to deliver.
Chapter 2 concludes with a discussion of how the motivations, plans for,
and achievement of the paperless office are bound up with myths about the
problems of paper, organizational symbols about change, and the need for
better understanding of the interplay between the technology of documents and the work practices they are part of. We describe our studies of
two very different organizations: one that successfully transformed its
work environment and one that did not.

In chapter 3 we present a case study of knowledge-based office work.
This study was important because it gave us a deep set of data about paper
use in a knowledge-intensive work environment at a variety of different levels: from organizational culture and values down to the more
detailed level of interaction in the work processes of these knowledge workers. It also gave us insights into a broad range of document
activities and the ways in which paper did or did not play a role in them.
This study was unique in that we were able to gather facts and figures on
paper use as well as rich descriptions of how paper was used in many different kinds of work activities. In many ways, it became the cornerstone of
future work and the benchmark against which our other studies were
compared.

For example, the case study led to a series of more detailed investigations into why people often prefer to read from paper rather than computer screens. After the study, we and our colleague Kenton O'Hara began
a series of studies examining work-related reading in more detail. In chapter 4 we describe this work, breaking down our observations into a number of different issues such as:

• The extent to which people mark up documents as they read, especially
when that reading is intense and reflective

• The importance of flexible navigation and manipulation of paper documents for a variety of reading activities

• The importance of laying out paper in space for reading, in order to read and write across documents

We show that reasons such as these go beyond the issues of screen resolution, contrast, and brightness. At this point we also also foreshadow some of the design implications that come from this work, which are more fully discussed in chapter 6.

In chapter 5, we look at the role of paper in collaborative work. By looking at three very different work settings—air traffic control, police officers on the beat, and office life in a chocolate manufacturing company—we discover how paper is used:

• As a tool for managing and coordinating action among co-workers in a shared environment

• As a medium for information gathering and exchange

• As an artifact in support of discussion

• As a means of archiving information for groups of co-workers

All three different kinds of workplaces show that the role of paper is much more complex and deeply interwoven with work practices than might at first appear. Each example highlights the fact that when an organization attempts to move away from paper, whatever the motivations behind doing so, it must understand what such a move will entail. Here we find that organizations undergoing change need to manage their own expectations as much as the process of change itself.

Chapter 6 pulls together many of the findings and shows how they can be applied to practical matters of design. It shows how understanding why and how paper is used in existing work processes can be a way of directing and inspiring the design of new technologies. We illustrate this with two major technology categories as examples: e-books (or digital reading devices) and document management systems. Here we highlight ways in which existing technologies provide affordances different from those of paper. We use these comparisons to suggest how these technologies might be changed to take advantage of the affordances of both the paper and digital worlds. We also discuss the need to develop technologies that attempt to better integrate paper use with coexisting digital technologies.

Finally, in chapter 7, we focus on what we see as paper's role in the future. We discuss the value of paper as a temporary or intermediary tool in a wide variety of activities in office life and explain why we think this will increasingly be a characteristic of how paper is used in the future. We also comment on where we can expect paper to be supplanted by digital technologies and what, technologically speaking, will be required in order for those changes to occur. We argue that paper will continue to occupy an important place in office life but will increasingly be used in conjunction with an array of electronic tools. This has at least two important implications. First, the designers and developers of new technologies need to accept and recognize the importance of paper in work-related activities and in organizational processes, and turn their attention from systems that replace paper to those that integrate the paper and electronic worlds. Second, organizations need to change their thinking in order to move effectively toward the future. Rather than pursuing the ideal of the paperless office, they should work toward a future in which paper and electronic document tools work in concert and in which organizational processes make the most of both worlds.

2
What's Wrong with Paper?

Figure 2.1 shows an office stuffed with paper: the desks and even the chairs are overflowing with files, reports, and articles. The irony here is that this is an office in a high-tech research laboratory. To make matters worse, this is a lab dedicated to research into new technologies to support office work. Staff are given large amounts of money to invest in the latest equipment and are expected to make full use of these new devices. Despite this, the office is full of paper.

This particular person's office created a problem for the senior managers of this high-tech lab. Interestingly, the managers' problem was not that the occupant of the office was ineffective or inefficient. (As it happened, this person was legendary for being able to lay his hands on any piece of paper or document he might need at a moment's notice.) Rather, their problem was what his office *said* about the lab. This was especially of concern to them whenever the CEO of their organization and his entourage visited. When such visits were looming, managers became very concerned that they make the right impression. In particular, they wanted to show that this was a workplace reaching out to the future rather than being trapped in an inefficient past. They wanted to demonstrate to their senior colleagues that the investments made in research were bearing fruit in a workplace that was inventing new technologies and that was itself new, innovative, and dynamic in taking on new forms of work process and in using the latest systems. Yet, if this individual's office was anything to go by, the reality was that this workplace of the future was full of paper. How could a research establishment attempting to invent the future succeed if it was tied down by technologies of the past?

Figure 2.1
The office of a manager at a high-tech research establishment.

To deal with this problem, the managers used quite a simple strategy: hide the paper. When a visit from higher-ups was imminent, the occupant of the offending office was obliged to remove all his paper documents and temporarily conceal them in boxes hidden in a cupboard under the stairwell. No matter that this would handicap the person's work or create havoc for the support staff; the paper had to go.

From time to time, this paper-hiding exercise would result in a major cleanup. Large piles of paper, on being returned to the office, would be sorted through, organized, and filed. Amazing quantities of paper would also be thrown out. For a brief time, the office would be transformed: large patches of the desk could now be seen and some semblance of order was achieved. But inevitably, and usually within a few weeks, it would return to its normal cluttered state.

This is more than a funny story. A more serious, consequential issue lies beneath it: in this organization, as elsewhere, people often measure things with symbols. Our anecdote of the paperful office shows that the problem of paper may symbolize other problems. To get rid of paper in an office is not always a question of getting rid of paper per se, but getting rid of whatever other problems paper signifies.

Many readers will be familiar from their own experiences of how paper comes to symbolize other things. Mostly such tales are about small matters, but the symbolic value of paper can be much more important than our tales might imply. Sometimes quite significant changes are brought about in organizations because of it. Some of these changes may ultimately prove to be beneficial, but some may not.

The Problem with Paper

Our concern in this chapter is to show that there are three different classes of problems that paper presents: *symbolic* problems, *cost* problems, and *interactional* problems. Our opening example highlights the symbolic problem with paper, and it is interesting to ask how this has come to be. Paper as a symbol of the old-fashioned past is rooted in some real issues having to do with costs and interactional limitations. In other words, paper is sometimes the more costly, less efficient, more cumbersome option when compared to new technologies. These are the kinds of problems document system consultants will point out to information technology (IT) managers. These are the facts and figures that organizations have in mind when they envision moving toward the office of the future.

We begin by describing some of the costs associated with paper and comparing them to costs in the digital world. These include the delivery, storage, and retrieval costs of paper-based versus electronic systems, and also less straightforward costs.

These costs in turn are related to the interactional limitations of paper. By interactional limitations we mean the limits imposed by the nature of paper as a physical medium for interaction: the fact that it is difficult to amend and revise, difficult to access remotely, and so forth. These are the issues to do with the affordances of paper, or more precisely those actions that paper does *not* afford.

Finally, we describe the cases of two organizations that attempted to move away from paper, in order to illustrate how the symbolic, the cost, and the interactional issues are often intermingled. In both cases, the idea of moving to a paperless future motivated change. A concern with the "problems" of paper came to symbolize a concern with how to move from an inefficient present to a gloriously efficient future. This symbolic concern was used to much different effect in these organizations, however. In the first case, it was used to create radical and effective change. In the second, it failed to achieve any real impact.

More specifically, we describe the case of a Danish design and manufacturing company that attempted—quite successfully as it turned out—to transform itself through a movement away from paper. Here the notion of going paperless was in essence a slogan used to motivate and publicize change, but the real intent was to transform work practices rather than to abandon paper for its own sake. Such a transformation could only be achieved by moving away from technologies that fixed people to time and place. Paper was one such technology because it meant that workers had to be near paper-filing cabinets.

We contrast the experience of this organization with another, this time a company based in the United Kingdom. This organization also used "going paperless" as a slogan to publicize change but failed to achieve success because the elimination of paper quickly became the goal rather than the by-product of efforts to change more fundamental problems in the work processes.

The lesson we take from these two studies is that what is perceived to be a problem with paper consists of an amalgam of concerns. Many of these concerns have little to do with paper itself. Sometimes preserving this amalgam can enable an organization to achieve its goals, sometimes it leads to failure, and sometimes it is better to disentangle these issues and focus on one of them. But, above all, it is important for organizations to be clear as to the actual cost or interactional problems they are concerned with. Without doing so, it is often difficult for an organization to define how its current work practices need changing and the role paper might play in the future. It is also difficult to pinpoint when paper is a symptom rather than a cause of problems in business processes. Paper can be a problem indeed, but not always the one it seems to be.

The Cost Problem

New technologies hold out great potential for changing the way people do their work. Whether we consider a small office or a large global organization, just how to leverage these new systems can be incredibly complicated. There are strong motivators for change, however, and saving money is one of the strongest. It is easy for managers to see some of the costs new systems might help alleviate. For example, it is not unusual for a company to fixate on the amount of paper storage space that a company has to pay for. But comparing paper and electronic document systems is quite complex because the issues involve not only the cost of materials, and the cost of the devices and systems that consume the materials, but all the considerable costs for maintaining such systems and the costs of training people to use them. A cost evaluation must also take into account all the "downstream" activities that have to do with documents after they have been created and used: the costs of delivering, distributing, processing, filing, storing, retrieving, and even destroying documents.

The Cost of Paper Document Systems

Paper document systems are best thought of as incurring costs in a backloaded and ongoing way. In other words, the costs of paper document systems far outweigh those of electronic systems *after* the point at which they are created: the actual printing cost (cost of materials) is insignificant compared with the cost of dealing with documents after printing. The best statistics come from analyzing the use of paper forms in business. Estimates are that about 83 percent of all business documents consist of forms. In the United States, businesses spend about $1 billion a year designing and printing forms. However, they spend $25–35 billion a year filing, storing, and retrieving those paper forms and an extra $65–85 billion over the entire life cycle of those documents maintaining, updating, and distributing them.[1] If we can believe these figures, the cost of dealing with paper forms after they are produced vastly outweighs the cost of producing them.

Key costs for paper document systems are for the delivery, storage, and retrieval of paper. For the delivery of even a single document, price differentials for paper and electronic media are substantial. The cost of sending a document by courier or even by regular mail is much higher than sending it as an e-mail attachment. For most of us, using e-mail is a cost that we rarely think about and that is hard to quantify. At worst, it is the cost of a local phone call. Posting a letter, on the other hand, is a more obvious cost, usually involving the actual handing over of money. That e-mail is cheaper is a fact most organizations recognize. For example, many organizations are actively trying to do away with paper-based faxing in favor of e-mail or electronic faxing, where documents are created electronically at the sending end.

The cost of delivery is a topic that the publishing industry is understandably concerned with. Here, differences in shipping costs can be seen directly in the price of publications like conference proceedings, which can be six times higher for the paper than for the CD-ROM version. Producing on CD-ROM is especially cost-effective for large numbers of documents. A 1996 case study found that because of shipping costs, producing and delivering five thousand 1,000-page documents on CD-ROM cost less than half as much as producing and delivering the paper version.[2]

Storage of paper is an even bigger cost issue for many organizations. Banks, law firms, and records offices require enormous amounts of space for their archives. Much of this is to preserve a paper trail of past actions and events. Every letter, every transaction is kept just in case it may ever be needed. In fact, most of these documents are never accessed and never needed. Some of these paper files are kept as a legal necessity. Many are kept because they provide a kind of emotional security blanket. In a study we undertook of a major confectionary firm, we found that office workers very rarely, if ever, accessed documents they kept in off-site storage facilities, yet they were loathe to throw these documents out. It is no wonder that filing cabinet manufacturers have been enjoying a continuing increase in sales.

The actual cost of storage space for paper is huge compared with digital storage. To store 2 million paper documents, an organization can expect to spend between $40,000 and $60,000 on filing cabinets alone. This doesn't even include the cost of floor space for the cabinets. This many paper documents can fit on fewer than ten CD-ROMs. An optical disc storage "jukebox" for CDs is less than the size of a small refrigerator and can replace about six hundred four-drawer filing cabinets. Digital storage costs and capacity change so rapidly that these figures may well be out-of-date by the time this book is published.

Related to this is the cost of filing and retrieving documents from these vast paper archives. There are some frightening statistics here. Estimates are that 3 percent of all paper documents are filed incorrectly, and almost

8 percent are eventually "lost."[3] A study of managers in the United States found that they spend an average of three hours a week looking for paper that has been misfiled, mislabeled, or lost. Altogether, the cost of misfiled documents is upward of $120 per document.[4] Compare this with the seconds it can take to search through a computer database for a file. Of course, it takes seconds if you know the right keyword or file name. Interestingly, we found no facts or figures indicating how much time people spend looking for electronic files or losing them altogether. But how many of us at some time or other have spent hours recovering files from system crashes, racking our brains for the name of an ancient file, or working on the wrong version of a file? Also, how many of those files can now not be accessed because they are in an old format or on a now obsolete kind of floppy disk or magnetic tape? As we say, the issues are more complex than many technology suppliers might suggest with their cost statistics.

However, if electronic files suffer obsolescence in the face of technological progress, paper documents incur costs through obsolescence in other ways. Paper documents become obsolete as the world marches on. In the conventional way of doing things, paper forms and other business documents are preprinted, often by offset printers, in centralized printshops and in large print runs. Many of these documents, such as forms, become out-of-date well before a stockpile can be used up. It is estimated that in the United States, one third of all forms are simply wasted because they are out-of-date before they are ever used.[5] Often, these useless materials are stored for long periods of time before they are thrown out; this costs more money. Related to this is the cost of workers such as technicians or service reps using paper manuals that are out-of-date. These costs, too, can be substantial.

Taking these issues into account, it is no surprise that there is a move away from centralized offset printing to digital on-demand printing. As we saw in chapter 1, on-demand printing allows people to print only what they need and to be sure of the most up-to-date form or manual.

The Cost of Digital Document Systems

The costs of digital document systems are much harder to specify. Partly this is because they tend to be up-front costs. That is, while it may be much cheaper to distribute and store electronic documents, it can be much more expensive to produce them. In the publishing industry, estimates are that electronic documents take 20–25 percent longer to produce than paper books. But these added costs are likely to disappear as we become more skilled in digital document design and creation, and as the cost of the technology needed to produce these documents comes down.

What will not disappear, however, is the price of change. First, there are the setup costs of moving from the old ways of working to the new. There is the cost of the equipment, which can be substantial. Then there is the time and effort required by organizations to choose which of the newest document systems will best suit their needs. These are not easy decisions. The outlay of money to purchase and install a new document system can be huge. Document system consultancies are a booming business because of this. These consultants analyze an organization's needs and either help choose off-the-shelf systems or put together customized solutions.

This is not to say that once the decision is made everyone will be happy. Training and changing the way people work are other big up-front costs. People do not always adjust happily or easily to new ways of working. In a study we conducted of a front office for an international manufacturing company, one full time member of staff, two consultants, and three students worked for a period of six months to select a new document system and to help convince the users that this would improve their business processes. By the end of that period, the company had not even begun to install the new system, and skeptics abounded.

The process of bringing about these changes also required that staff members take time out from their hectic schedules to sort through all the paper they kept on site in preparation for scanning into the new system. Partly this was necessary to make the vision of the office of the future work. For if electronic document systems would help the organization to "liberate" knowledge from the filing cabinets and make it accessible to all, this required each person to make a judgment about what was worth keeping in the long term, as well as how to categorize that knowledge. For a small sample of workers a procedure was put in place whereby they were encouraged to sort through their paper files for scanning into the new document management system. This procedure took weeks to complete. Each person understandably had many more important concerns than doing this kind of "housekeeping" chore. Even more disappointing for this "office of the future" task force was that, when all was said and done, these office workers set aside only 7 percent of their paper documents for scanning. A large number of them (38 percent) they chose to keep on or near their desks in paper form.

This is but one example; we could list many more. The point is, whenever a transition to new ways of working takes place, it takes time and money. And for some people, the new ways may never be seen to be as good as the old ways of working. In the United Kingdom, for example, we have recently seen the cost of transition. Partly as a result of the installation of a new computerized system, the passport office experienced a huge backlog of applications. Hundreds of extra people had to be hired to deal with the backlog, massive queues formed outside the regional offices, and rules had to be relaxed to speed the process. This transitional phase created such a national furor, with thousands of people worried about their vacations abroad, that it reached national government levels and statements were made to the House of Commons. Many called for a return to the previous paper-based process. After all, they argued, at least it worked. So change has its price, and this may not simply be in the cost of new systems. But costs are not the only problem pertinent to the role of paper. As we have remarked, there are interactional ones, too. It is to those we now turn.

The Interactional Problem

In chapter 1 we talked about the ways in which we can view paper as an artifact that shapes interaction, that allows certain actions and not others. Because of its very nature, there are things you can do with it and things you cannot. The limits that paper places on how it can be used are as follows:

• Paper must be used locally and cannot (without supporting technology) be remotely accessed.

• Paper occupies physical space and thus requires space for its use and storage. Vast amounts of paper require vast amounts of storage space.

• Paper requires physical delivery.

• A single paper document can be used by only one person at a time (or, at least, if shared, this significantly changes the way it is used).

• Paper documents cannot be easily revised, reformatted, and incorporated into other documents.

• Paper documents cannot be easily replicated (without the help of photocopiers, scanners, etc).

• Paper documents, on their own, can be used only for the display of static, visual markings. They cannot display moving images or play sounds (without technological assistance).

These limitations are all the more salient in contrast to the kinds of actions electronic documents allow. Providing you have the right supporting system and infrastructure, the location of an electronic document does not matter. You bring the document to your computer rather than bringing yourself to the document. In terms of space required for using and storing electronic documents, the limits are imposed by the size of display screen and the space occupied by the computer on your desk. For most of us, storage space is not an issue—it is often done centrally via a network. In any case, computer storage will never take up as much space as all the paper we keep. Electronic documents do not require physical delivery: they can be transmitted rather than carried. With electronic documents you can easily edit, rearrange, reformat, or replicate a document. Furthermore, you can do all this to a document at the same time someone else can. Finally, you can create or display multimedia documents: mixtures of text, scene, moving image, and sound.

This all seems quite straightforward. It is no wonder that paper is viewed as a technology of the past. There are many limits on what you can do with it, and these are reflected directly in terms of real costs: not only the money it takes to store, deliver, and manage paper but the opportunity costs in terms of the efficiency and productivity that new document systems might deliver. As we discuss later, each of these so-called interactional limitations can be turned on its head. For each limit, for each set of actions that paper prevents, there is a set of actions that it enables. In other words, each limitation is also an affordance. This we saw in our studies of different work settings and different kinds of tasks. Unfortunately, it is not always clear whether the interactional limitations of paper versus electronic media are in fact causing problems for organizations or whether there are other issues afoot (which may have little to do with paper). This is another way of saying that real life is more complicated, much richer, and much more interesting than any simple comparison of paper and electronic media would indicate.

Two Case Studies

Though the precise affordances of paper (whether "good" or "bad") may be difficult to specify, there are then often good reasons why organizations want to replace paper with digital alternatives. Reducing the cost of paper is perhaps the most obvious good reason. There are also real interactional limitations as well as symbolic issues (such as that paper can signify to others that an organization is backward-looking).

At the outset of this chapter we saw that one difficulty here is that these issues can get muddled up. When organizations attempt change, they aren't always certain whether they simply want to be seen to be reaching for the future or really want to reduce costs. Quite often they may have little or no idea of what interactional limitations paper may be imposing on them. Nonetheless, organizations bravely launch themselves into the process of change hopeful that by the end they will be better for it. Unfortunately, this is not always the case. We finish this chapter by looking at how two companies tried to change their ways of working by altering the underlying technologies in support of that work. These changes revolved around all three of the different classes of problem that we have described: the symbolic, the cost, and the interactional. We see how one organization succeeded and the other did not, and perhaps more important, the ways in which the issues are often subtly interconnected.

The Case of DanTech

Much of the research we have done over the years has involved observations of real organizations. In the course of doing this, we have become increasingly convinced that the paperless office is truly a myth. Wherever we went, paper seemed to be stacked wall-to-wall, in every office and in every kind of organization: hospitals, financial institutions, research laboratories, telecommunications companies, to name but a few. We were therefore understandably intrigued to hear about the existence of a paperless office in Copenhagen, at the headquarters of an organization (which we call DanTech) that leads the world in its particular domain of manufacturing and design for a high-tech product. Indeed, because of its apparent uniqueness, DanTech had received a significant amount of press attention. One article we saw showed a picture of a shiny office with desks free of the usual clutter of paper and documents we see in most offices.

We were therefore grateful to be allowed to visit this organization to learn for ourselves what was the nature of this "office of the future." We did learn many interesting lessons, not so much about the paperless office as about the process of organizational change and the role of technology in supporting that change.

A Brief History of DanTech   We start by briefly sketching the history of DanTech, why it wanted to change, and how it set about doing so. Established at the turn of the century, this Danish organization was the world's oldest in its business area and, at the time of our visit, the most successful. But it was not always the world leader. In the 1970s it fell behind U.S. manufacturers, who took the lead in developing new technology. During the 1980s, DanTech decided that radical new steps were necessary to regain its market share. At the end of the decade, new management began to implement major organizational changes in an attempt to set the pace for the industry and to stay ahead of competitors.

To achieve this, DanTech decided to do away completely with old organizational structures and implement new ones. Key to these new processes was the decision to reorganize work processes around small interdisciplinary project teams configured specifically for the projects at hand. Further, each person on a team would be trained to do at least two jobs, thereby increasing the flexibility with which teams could be reconfigured. It was also decided that in order for these project teams to work effectively, it was essential that team members be co-located not just at the same work site, but as clusters of people working at desks next to each other. This, it was thought, would maximize productivity and efficiency. Thus, the new work processes emphasized flexibility and mobility, prerequisites, it was believed, if project teams were to be put together as and when needed.

Two practical steps were necessary to implement these changes. First, it was necessary to move to a new site—a site that was custom-built to support and reflect the new work processes. Second, it was necessary to provide technological tools to support the mobility of project teams within the building. A side effect of this was to put strict limits on the amount of paper that any one person kept. As in all organizations, paper acts as a kind of organizational anchor, tying individuals to the physical location of their documents. If this anchor could be dissolved without removing access to these documents, the physical mobility of staff within the organization could be achieved. Accordingly, it was not that DanTech intended to go paperless but rather that it wanted to restrict the amount of paper that was stored. It was this that motivated the adoption of the paperless office slogan by DanTech's managers.

DanTech managers had several requirements for their new building. They wanted an open-plan office with generic desks that no one person would own for the long term. Rather, each employee would occupy one desk only for the duration of a project. The office building would also do away with office spaces reflecting any sort of hierarchy—so, for example, the CEO would occupy a desk much like any other person in the company. In order to maximize interaction among employees, walls and enclosed spaces would be kept to a minimum. However, a small set of rooms would be provided for private phone calls, small meetings, and conferences. In keeping with the idea of facilitating proximity among workers and recognizing the importance of informal meetings, coffee stations would be provided in central locations on each floor. Employees would also be discouraged from using the elevators, in order to encourage chance encounters and conversations in the course of using the stairs.

In doing away with the conventional organization of an office, the aim was to provide each employee with an electronic office that moved as the employee moved from desk to desk. Key to this new environment would be the design of an effective electronic filing system. Specific technological requirements were to be determined by a series of interviews with employees to specify what sort of databases and tools they would need.

As for paper, each project team was to be limited to one set of hanging file folders on a mobile trolley. Paper mail was to be scanned in and then shredded, with the exception of paper documents that needed to be kept for legal purposes. These were to be stored in a central vault. The shredded paper was to be disposed of down a translucent plastic chute. This chute was to be translucent deliberately, so that everyone could see the paper being "done away with." The chute would also run vertically down the wall of the cafeteria—the most public place in the building.

DanTech's Experiences   We visited DanTech some eighteen months after this program of change had commenced. At this time, DanTech's IT manager told us that the single most important factor in helping to bring about radical organizational change at DanTech had been the move away from the old site to a new building. This building, though turn-of-the-century, had been completely gutted and restructured internally for the purpose. This refurbished building in a well-to-do region of Copenhagen looked like many other elegant, period buildings from the outside. But within, it was unlike any other. Gleaming wooden floors and soft lighting were combined with open spaces that effectively prevented its taking on a warehouse-like atmosphere—a complaint with many open-plan offices. Indeed the effect was quite the reverse. Each part of the building had a unique identity, yet there were very few walls or barriers. The overall effect was a relaxed, informal atmosphere.

The desks, for the most part, were uncluttered by the usual paraphernalia of normal office life: there were computers on all, but only some telephones—employees were gradually being equipped with mobile phones. Perhaps more noticeably there were no large stacks of paper, no in and out trays, and very few files in evidence. There was paper, to be sure, but its existence did not appear to overwhelm or intrude into the office space as it often does in other environments. There were none of those "problem paper" documents that one sees in most organizations: heaped up, pushed aside, and apparently forgotten. Instead, what paper was being used looked as if it were providing an immediate practical function: it was being used to write on, to read from, or for a team to sit around and discuss.

With regard to new technologies, the tools that the organization provided on any employee's "electronic desk" were in fact quite minimal. On each person's PC, the electronic desktop gave access to a word processor, a spreadsheet tool, a calendar, e-mail facilities, and an electronic filing system.

As it happened, it was the selection and design of the electronic filing system that presented the greatest challenge for the IT management team.

When employees were asked what kinds of data they would like access to, and how they should be organized, everyone had different ideas. The planned system fast became overly complex.

As an initial solution, preexisting shared databases were left as they were, and if these existed in paper form, they were also left untouched and placed in a centrally accessible location. For the documents that employees themselves produced, the IT managers provided a very flexible system, allowing people to organize their own filing systems using the concepts of electronic shelves and binders. However, they vastly overestimated people's ability to do this. With no structure at all, people found it very difficult to categorize their documents and often got lost in their own filing systems.

As a second attempt, the IT managers ordered a system with a very simple structure: each project group was to have a system with about ten different filing "boxes" corresponding to documents associated with different phases of each project, beginning with "specification" through to "final documents." Only project leaders could alter this basic structure. To protect against misfiling or problems with categorization, people were encouraged to provide good file names and key words for each document. Access rights to the files were initially under the control of project team members, but these were rarely used, or people forgot to change them, so eventually they were done away with altogether.

This second approach with a simplified, project-based filing structure turned out to be successful and is the one used today. Some of this success was attributed to the fact that team members had a primary requirement only for accessing documents that were, as a matter of course, related to the project they were currently working on (namely, design specifications, prototype reports, marketing analyses, and the like). There seemed to be little requirement for the retrieval of documents related to other people's projects or to already completed projects.

DanTech's Use of Paper So, was DanTech a paperless office? No, although what this organization had successfully done was to drastically reduce the amount of paper that was used and stored. Its experience, however, offers important insights into how and where paper finds a place in work.

First, paper continued to play a key role in the support of current work or work in progress. Most of the documents of central importance to an ongoing project existed on paper, at least for some short period of time. Documents were often printed in order to be read, to be marked up, or to be referred to while authoring other documents. They were often arrayed upon the desktop, as a way of temporarily marshaling, organizing, displaying, and giving access to information, and as a way of reminding workers of jobs that needed to be done or things that needed attending to.

Furthermore, once many of these documents had served their purpose in paper form, there was no need to keep them in the longer term in any form (i.e., electronically or on paper). DanTech found this surprising at first.

For example, in the initial stages of organizational change, DanTech attempted to scan all its paper mail. One person was put in charge of scanning and then shredding any incoming paper. However, it was soon discovered that, for many letters, keeping electronic copies was unnecessary. Many of them were only useful for short-term purposes, and these purposes were best served by keeping the documents in paper form. Letters announcing impending visitors or upcoming conferences and meetings were best illustrative of this. In being left in paper form, they could be left on a desktop to act as tangible reminders or displayed on a notice board to be seen by anyone interested. DanTech found that most letters were like this and that the bulk of mail was not suited to long-term electronic storage.

But DanTech had not expected the same to hold true for what it called its design process documents. These were the documents that recorded the process of design and development, consisting mainly of written records of decisions, analysis, and reports of testing as well as design specifications and drawings. It was thought that these documents constituted DanTech's "organizational memory" and that, accordingly, they needed to be kept. Electronic means would make such storage cheap and retrieval easy. But, again to their surprise, DanTech managers discovered that the bulk of these documents only had a life during the design process itself, and like much of the incoming post, they needed to be at hand and in paper form during that process. As the work progressed, these documents became less and less important, losing life as time passed by. In terms of using these documents to trace decisions and aid recollection in future design processes, DanTech found that they were hardly ever reused or retrieved. This is not because DanTech did not learn from its design processes and constantly endeavor to improve; it was rather that the learning and knowledge were embedded in the minds of DanTech's design staff, not in the documents those individuals produced. In other words, despite the managers' best efforts to leverage the knowledge in their documentation, ultimately the knowledge resided in the minds of the engineers.

Lessons from DanTech   The success and learning of DanTech teach us at least a couple of lessons about the symbolic, cost, and interactional problems of paper. The most important lesson is that DanTech fully recognized that "going paperless" was a *symbol of change* rather than a *cause of change*. DanTech's IT managers did not stick dogmatically to notions about reducing paper but rather recognized that getting rid of paper was not always a sensible end in itself. Their focus instead was on changing their underlying work processes, whether through restructuring the processes themselves, changing the physical environment, or changing the artifacts and technologies supporting those processes, including paper. There were some attempts to make changes that failed (such as scanning in all paper mail), but they learned from these failures and adapted them accordingly. Hence, by remaining open-minded, the managers at DanTech in effect disentangled the symbolic from the real problems associated with paper. By doing so, they were able to identify what could be leveraged through a move toward a paperless environment.

A second important lesson is that DanTech was able to use the symbolic value of paper to marshal and motivate change. Staff members were encouraged to think deeply about which documents they really needed and in what form; they were forced to think about which documents they really needed to have stored. What they then discovered were some unexpected things, such as the fact that the use of documents in ongoing work was different from the use of documents for completed work. Documents were far more important when they were part of the living process of design than when a project had been completed. When workers moved on to a new project, the knowledge was in their heads, not in the documents. It is no wonder, then, that leveraging this knowledge was best done by bringing together effective project teams as and when necessary. The managers were free to do this within the new organizational and environmental structures that DanTech had introduced.

Externally, the organization was also able to leverage the symbolic move toward a less papercentric organization. Media publicity helped to differentiate it in the marketplace and to highlight its dynamic, forward-looking nature. This helped the profile of its products. Indeed, the amount of publicity the company received about being paperless was enormous, and its value was perceived to far outweigh the fact that it somewhat misrepresented the truth.

All these changes were, of course, not without their real costs. Moving to a new, custom-made building was an enormously expensive undertaking. Early implementations of a much more extensive electronic archive than was needed also cost money, as did the iterative process used to arrive at a better solution. To complicate matters, the costs of the new products DanTech developed during this period were very much higher than the costs for products in previous periods. This was not because of the changes in work practices or the move to the paperless office. This reflected the greater costs of digital versus mechanical technologies to which DanTech shifted during this period. The new products were more complicated, more precise, and more sophisticated. The overall cost of change was therefore very difficult to measure.

On the savings side, however, the move to a less papercentric environment had to do primarily with the bulk and volume of paper kept on site. But what is more significant than how much money this saved was the interactional consequences of the move to reduce paper storage. The sheer bulk of paper had prevented the physical reconfiguration of working teams. Paper had acted as an anchor for DanTech's staff members, tying them to particular filing cabinets and desks within the organization. Electronic alternatives broke these shackles and facilitated DanTech's new work processes. This was the most important benefit that was achieved with the reduction of paper.

The Case of UKCom
Competitive pressures forced DanTech to change. Transformations in the work environment, in patterns of team work, and in the infrastructure that supported that work helped achieve those changes. The slogan "the paper-

less office" was used to symbolize those concerns and help motivate the workforce. Invoking the ideal of the paperless office as the motivator of change is not always so successful, however. Another large organization we looked at (a telecommunications company based in the United Kingdom, which we call UKCom) is a case in point. Here the removal of paper distracted attention away from other important aspects of change rather than helping draw attention to them.

A Brief History of UKCom   Again, we start with the background to these changes. Until the late 1980s, UKCom was one of the two main players in a specialized telecommunications installations business. Throughout the 1970s and early 1980s the marketplace began to shrink. At the same time there was a shift from what UKCom sometimes called "dumb technologies" to more advanced digital approaches to their business. At the end of the 1980s, radical changes in its parent company forced UKCom to merge with a smaller U.K. rival. This merger, combined with changing products and diminishing business opportunities, forced UKCom to reassess its processes.

UKCom managers decided they needed new ways of working. They decided that a move toward a paperless office would provide a focus that would help identify and enable these ways. They began by setting up a paperless task force, which identified some key areas of the business and key processes in which to begin to make these changes. They settled on the Bids and Sales department. Bids and Sales was a department responsible for putting together bids (traditionally very large and quite complex paper documents outlining conditions and costs for installing new telecommunications systems) in response to calls for tender by its customers (usually large consortia). One reason for choosing this as a starting place was that Bids and Sales was very much seen as the hub of the organization: the interface to its customers and the department with which most other departments interacted. Within Bids and Sales, the task force began by identifying two main areas where a move away from paper toward digital alternatives might bring noticeable benefits.

The first area was that of customer account management. Here, the task force believed, this process could be improved if it used document technologies that allowed remote access. Up to that time, this had been mostly paper-based, which restricted document access to one person at a time, one place at a time. The second area had to do with the process of calculating costs. Here using paper was viewed as a potential problem because information on paper could not be updated when new costs had to be calculated. In other words, paper fixed information, and what was required was information that could be easily manipulated and modified.

Plan 1: Change the process for account managers   UKCom tracked customer needs through account managers. Account managers were essentially experts on customers. Their job was to elicit from customers (over a period of months and even years) requirements for both current and future installations. These requirements might include anything from technical details for installations to price ranges that would be acceptable to such issues as who might be members of the consortia UKCom would be dealing with. Account managers would share this information with the UKCom head office as and when they saw fit or in meetings specifically arranged for the purpose. Traditionally, account managers would document their customer information on paper and share this at occasional meetings with the Bids and Sales department.

But changes in the marketplace meant that this way of working was no longer as effective as it had been. One reason was that account managers were playing a more important role than they had been. In earlier decades, account managers were essentially one-way conduits for information from the customer to UKCom. By the early 1990s, however, there needed to be a two-way exchange of information. This involved giving feedback to customers so that they could be made more aware of the "intelligent" options available to them. In other words, account managers needed to share information about customer needs with Bids and Sales in real time. They also needed to get information about new technological possibilities back to the customers as soon as information was available. Unfortunately, this was made difficult by the fact that changes in the marketplace also meant that account managers spent more and more time traveling.

UKCom managers believed that a move away from paper and toward new digital devices would help solve these problems. Foremost in their minds was the introduction of a new electronic document database combined with portable hardware. The database would allow the account managers to enter customer information that could be shared with their colleagues back at headquarters. In turn, Bids and Sales staff could enter information about the latest technology offerings that might satisfy customer needs. New hardware, consisting of a mix of laptops, palm-tops, and mobile phones, would offer the account managers remote access to this database wherever they were. The hope was that adopting these new technologies would lead account managers to abandon their long treasured paper notebooks—one small step toward the paperless office.

Plan 2: Change the process for putting together bids   The second area in which the paperless task force thought improvements could be made had to do with putting together the projected costs for the bid document. Traditionally, projected costs for an installation were calculated by individual departments and delivered to the Bids and Sales department as a paper-based summary. This was then incorporated into the main document by the Bids and Sales department. A major problem was that integration of figures that came from different kinds of spreadsheets was not an easy or straightforward task because each department had its own way of doing spreadsheets and estimating costs. Making this process electronic, it was thought, would greatly speed the turnaround time for putting a bid together. A centralized electronic application accessible to all departments would automatically ensure that the enormous number of variables that needed to be considered would be taken into account. When changes had to be made, the figures could automatically be updated. In addition, a database that integrated all the divisional databases would create standardization across departments. And finally, such a system would allow the central office to track actual costs against these projected estimates. This would allow UKCom to better see where any inaccuracies were coming from and to learn from past experience.

UKCom's Experience   The introduction of these new systems for both the account managers and for budgeting and planning was expected to cause considerable havoc at first, especially in the case of the new integrated database to be implemented across departments. Some resistance from staff was also expected until they became familiar with what the new technology could do. Account managers in particular were expected to be less than keen, since they would have to shift their working habits away from being very much pen-and-paper-based toward a system that required them to enter and use data online.

As it turned out, there were fewer technological problems than expected, but more resistance from staff. More than this, the grounds for people's resistance were a surprise. For example, the technical problem of constructing a customer database with an interface that would be acceptable to both the account managers and to staff in Bids and Sales turned out to be much easier than expected. Everyone liked the graphical interface. They also liked the fact that they could enter text in a relatively free and easy way. However, the information entered by the account managers into this new customer database was a great disappointment. To begin with, much less information was entered than had been expected by the head office. It was also rather general, not to say vague, and any special details that would enable UKCom to get a better understanding of customer requirements seemed to be entirely lacking from the database until immediately before a call for contract was made.

The account managers explained that the reason for this was that their work revolved around "relations management." By this they meant that the most important part of their work involved cultivating personal relationships with their contacts in the customer organizations. Mostly this was done in face-to-face meetings, and often through wining and dining (hence, account managers were sometimes called "claret swiggers"). It was these contacts who provided the kind of details that account managers would enter at the last minute. More important, these contacts would also provide what account managers called "trusted gateways" to key decision makers. Such trusted gateways were especially important when trying to create a two-way process of information exchange in the new business environment.

The account managers explained that they believed most of this information (often kept in their notebooks) was unsuited for sharing. For example, some of this information would consist of lists of the leisure activities of contacts. In other cases it would consist of biographical details about a contact's career within the customer organization. Some account managers even kept notes on people they would prefer *not* to deal with in the customer organization. Account managers insisted that this information was essentially subjective, and if posted on an electronic database, it could potentially be seen as libelous. In any case, account managers explained that this information was more or less unusable by anyone except themselves. Hence they continued to use their paper notebooks to store such information, not the newly created customer database.

On the other hand, the introduction of the new customer database and portable hardware did have some positive effects. Account managers found that they were able to become more up-to-date with technical possibilities through accessing the newly created intranet. Doing so involved not just reading the latest technical paper entered onto the database but also participating in the lively discussions with colleagues on electronic bulletin boards. A side benefit was also to make account managers feel closer to their colleagues in Bids and Sales.

Taken as a whole, however, the introduction of the new system did not achieve the beneficial effects expected. Whereas a move away from paper was expected to allow information sharing and access between account managers and Bids and Sales, the process ended up being only one-way, with account managers usually taking and not giving information via the network. That they did so was because of the nature of their job. In other words, the fact that the old paper-based ways of working did not allow remote access to information was not the key problem. Rather, it was the nature of the work practices themselves.

Much like the attempts to change the account management process, changes in budgets and planning also failed to deliver all the expected benefits. There was an overall reduction in the amount of paper used in this process. Most, if not all, of the divisions started delivering their cost projections in electronic form. But again there was significant resistance to the new system.

As an example, it turned out that the ambiguities and idiosyncrasies in the accounting processes of the various departments were made use of by some key participants in the process: namely installation managers. Installation managers were responsible at the end of an installation for making sure a project came in at or under budget. Under the old ways of working, the projected costs offered a certain amount of flexibility in the assignment of costs. This allowed the installation managers to shift funds from one code to another to deal with unpredicted costs. Similarly, these managers resisted the creation of an integrated system because the ultimate goal of tracking costs was to lessen the gap between actual and estimated costs. It turned out that installation managers actually benefited from this gap. In particular, they benefited by overestimating costs. Managers who brought projects in under these estimates were seen in a better light than those who overspent, irrespective of the total profit made on any installation. The result of a feedback loop that made the fit between estimates and actual expenditures closer would be that the actual profits made on any installation might be reduced. The paperless task force viewed this as a demonstration of a more effective and tightly run organization, but installation managers had a quite different view. And though the paperless office task force members might try, they were unable to persuade installation managers to think otherwise.

To sum up, in UKCom it became clear to the paperless task force that the work practices of the different people involved would need to change if the power of the new networked systems was to be fully leveraged. This included not only the way they did their jobs but also (in the case of the installation managers) the way they were assessed and held accountable for their work. Now, in DanTech, management had recognized that the changes it was trying to bring about with the move to paperlessness would be likely to entail radical changes in work practices. They were also in a position to make such changes. Unfortunately, in UKCom, the task force had no authority to direct or cause such changes to happen.

Lessons from UKCom   The lessons from UKCom are not simply that the organization misunderstood what could be achieved with a move toward a paperless environment. They have to do with how the problems and processes affected by such changes were much more complex and far-reaching than UKCom had initially recognized. Motivations for moving toward a paperless office were firmly based in the belief that moving away from paper would have both interactional and cost benefits. This was a reasonable up-front rationale. In parallel, the symbolic power of going paperless was leveraged by attempts on the part of the task force to advertise "going paperless" through whiteboard and coffee mugs printed with the slogan, and through "open days" where new systems were demonstrated.

What UKCom seemed to repeatedly come up against was resistance to change, people's clinging to the old ways of working. This was because the company began by focusing on the interactional limitations of paper as the problem. The managers believed that by making the paper-based process electronic, the underlying work processes would change for the better. For example, UKCom's task force was quite right to think that information held only on paper limited sharing of that information. What it failed to recognize, however, was that the information account managers kept was specifically unsuited to the kind of sharing and broadcasting that the electronic medium provided. If the task force wanted to change the way that account managers shared, it would need to change the underlying work processes, not the technology.

A similar lesson can be learned from the attempt to introduce the centralized electronic budget and planning system. Here again the task force focused on the interactional limitations of a fragmented paper-based accounting system. In its view, unnecessary costs were incurred by a system that depended on paper and the provision of static rather than dynamically updated information. Paper meant that the system was inaccurate and inefficient. The move to an electronic alternative was meant to integrate the system as well as to reduce the hours required to undertake the budget and planning processes. What the task force found was that work practices had evolved hand-in-hand with the paper-based system. Changing to an electronic system was bound to meet resistance unless the underlying work practices were altered first. Organizational structures and organizational culture needed to be confronted and understood before new systems could be successfully imposed.

What we see in the case of UKCom is an interesting contrast with DanTech. At DanTech, organizational change began by managers' looking at the underlying work processes and examining first and foremost how these could change. Support for that change was then reflected in changes that needed to be made to the physical working environment and the tools to support the new work processes. The symbolic power of going paperless was then leveraged only after the fact and was recognized for what it was: only a symbol of deeper changes that were taking place. In the case of UKCom, the up-front focus was on getting rid of paper. Paper was duly frowned upon by the task force and became the focus for change.

Electronic systems were seen as good and paper as bad. Work processes were seen as tied by paper: they only needed liberating through the new electronic systems to change for the better. In fact, it was the work processes that needed to change before paper could be done away with. At UKCom, the move toward a paperless environment was therefore much less successful than in DanTech. On the positive side, in the course of its attempts, UKCom did gain a deeper understanding of its own work processes. On the whole, however, the paperless task force found that it had to fight a difficult, uphill battle.

Conclusion

Paper can be a problem in organizational life, but not always the problem that is expected. We have seen that there are real problems of paper related both to costs and the interactional limitations of paper as an artifact or medium for supporting work. But we have also seen that these problems are often entwined with other issues, especially related to work practices and organizational value systems. This can lead to confusion. The problem of paper can get mistaken for the problem of inefficient work practices; inefficient work practices get accounted for by pointing to the limitations of paper. In these situations, paper is seen to symbolize an old-fashioned past, and a move away from it is viewed, rightly or wrongly, as a move toward a more efficient and effective future. The real issue for organizations, however, is not to get rid of paper for its own sake but to have sufficient motivation to understand their own work processes and the ways in which paper plays a role. Organizations can sometimes be distracted and confused when symbolic issues get bundled up with other issues and when they try to eliminate paper just for the sake of it.

In any organization, then, the need to constantly improve and enhance technologies and associated processes should not be undertaken without due regard to these kinds of complexities. Those leading such change need to avoid the mindset that says they should do away with paper at all costs. What this chapter suggests is that organizations need to think first in terms of how the fundamental work processes might be changed, and only then think how tools and technologies, including paper, might best support these processes. This would seem an obvious recommendation, and doubtless many organizations would claim that this is indeed what they do. Though we have presented just two case studies, our research in numerous other organizations over the past few years shows that this is not usually the case. Rather, we have seen more cases of failure than success when organizations look at paper before they look at anything else. It is no wonder, then, that the paperless office is rarely achieved. It is a difficult business to impose new technologies on ingrained, incumbent work practices that depend on paper in complicated ways. In the long run it may be easier for new technologies and new practices to develop and adapt to each other simultaneously. Part and parcel of this is understanding the affordances of paper as well as digital systems in terms of those work practices. A better understanding is what we hope to impart.

3

Paper in Knowledge Work

One of the great changes of the past few decades has been the shift away from manufactured goods toward knowledge-based products and services. Whereas our grandparents may have worked in factories making anything from ships to textiles, today we are more likely to work in an office where we use our skills to produce and analyze information. Key to this transformation has been the emergence of new technologies, especially digital technologies, that allow us to construct, display, relay, and analyze information at speeds and in volumes that we could hardly have imagined just a couple of decades ago. Today, even on mass production lines, such technologies are becoming ubiquitous. Workers are less likely to be using their hands and more likely to be using their minds to monitor, manage, and control the flow of information. There are now more knowledge-based activities within organizations than ever before. In the United States, for example, it was estimated that in 1995, 31 percent of the workforce could be labeled "knowledge workers."[1] Predictions are that the proportion of work that is knowledge-based will continue to increase significantly into the new millennium.

This has all sorts of interesting consequences: one is that training and education need to be different. Whereas before they often focused on the development of manual skills, there is now greater emphasis on mental skills. Becoming a knowledge worker means becoming expert in making professional judgments about a specific domain. This is the value in what knowledge workers do and is what they get paid for. Another consequence has to do with where knowledge workers do their work. There is not necessarily a need for knowledge workers to sit side-by-side, or to be in a specific place to do the work that they do. Very often they can work wherever they can access information. This is evidenced by the increasing popularity of teleworking. Employers, too, have recognized the benefits of this. Virtual teams are employed to work together despite the fact that individual members may be far from one another and indeed may never meet face-to-face.[2]

To fully leverage the skills of their knowledge workers, organizations spend increasingly large amounts of time and money investigating how that work may be more effectively supported. It is not simply a case of giving workers a computer and links to a network. Software applications need to be tailored to their specific needs. Hardware needs to be carefully chosen to enhance their productivity. And, as we saw in chapter 2, work practices need to be developed and refined so as to make best use of these new technologies.

It was precisely this concern that led us to an in-depth case study of a knowledge-based workplace for Xerox, for whom we were both working at the time. Xerox wanted to better understand the role technologies have in knowledge work (not only its own technologies but any kind of information technology) and wanted insights into what new products might be developed to support that work. The place we chose to look at was the International Monetary Fund (IMF) in Washington, D.C.

There are many reasons why we chose the IMF. Admittedly, not least among these was the fact that no outsider had ever been privy to the details of what goes on within the IMF.[3] More important, though, we discovered that despite the fact that the IMF was technology-rich and its staff was provided with the most up-to-date equipment, paper was still everywhere and in large quantities. Indeed, evidence suggested that paper consumption had increased with the passing of time. It was not simply that the organization was burdened with a legacy of paper. Rather, we found that paper played an important role alongside their new technologies.

In looking more closely at the role paper was playing, we kept coming back to the IMF's knowledge workers—mainly, the IMF's economists. They became the central focus of our enquiries. We interviewed them, watched them, asked them to keep a diary of the documents and tools that they used in their work, and one of us even went on a mission with them. The result was a rich set of data containing both descriptions of the things they did and facts and figures that gave us an overall picture of what went on. Taken together, these provided new insight into the nature of knowledge work and the role paper played in it.

To be more specific, it led us to discover that paper supports at least five important aspects of knowledge work:

1. It supports authoring work—although knowledge workers use electronic technologies when they are composing documents, paper is a key part of this process alongside the computer. They may draft documents electronically, but they show an overwhelming need to refer to paper as they do so.

2. Knowledge workers review documents on paper, especially their colleagues' work. They read it reflectively on paper, and annotate and comment on it as they do so. They do so despite the fact that they could do this on their computers.

3. When they plan and think about their projects and activities, they use pen and paper as the primary means of organizing the work and writing the plans.

4. Paper supports their collaborative activities: they sit at conference tables and go through a hard copy of the reports they are working on. They juxtapose sheets of paper and make marks on their documents in the course of their discussions.

5. Paper helps knowledge workers grease the wheels of organizational communication. Whenever an important document needs to be shared, knowledge workers will print out a hard copy and hand-deliver it themselves to their colleagues rather than send it electronically.

Our purpose in this chapter is to explain why this is so. To do this we look at such things as how much time these knowledge workers spent with documents, how much time they spent with each other, and how much of their work was spent with paper in hand. We also look at how much time they spent in particular kinds of activities because these facts, too, are relevant to understanding why paper was so important to them. These findings are important in chapter 6, when we see that a focus on paper helps us understand not only what paper can do but how digital technologies might do things better.

Background

Any study of modern working life needs to place knowledge work at its center. We could have chosen numerous places to carry out such a study, but the IMF was particularly appealing. For although the IMF is typical of large, complex organizations in its mix of activities (including clerical, administrative, and managerial work), knowledge-based work lies at the heart of what the IMF does.

The IMF is, in essence, a financial "club" to which virtually all the countries in the world belong. These member countries, as they are called, are obliged to pool resources, which are then used to provide low-interest loans to any member that finds itself in a balance-of-payments crisis.

Housed in a rather nondescript building a few blocks from the White House, the IMF (at the time of our study) had some three thousand staff members, of whom nine hundred were professional economists. It is these individuals who are the IMF's knowledge workers. One of the primary jobs of these economists is to analyze the circumstances that lead to balance-of-payments crises for their member countries and to determine criteria for the making of loans. They are also employed to analyze various financial questions put by the IMF's clients (who are various governments around the world). These questions could range from investigations into the effect of inflation on investment strategies to the effect of regulations on economic growth.

The main method for presenting their analyses is through written reports, although these are supported by verbal presentations. Most work tasks are completed within a cycle of three months, although some can take as long as six months. To give an idea of the scale of document activities, the IMF produced about forty-five hundred reports in the period of our six-month study. Since that period, its workload has increased even more. It is a very busy place indeed.

Also of particular interest to us was the fact that the IMF is technology-rich, with high levels of investment in information technology (IT). At the time of our study, the IMF was spending about $18,000 a year per member of staff on IT and support services, and in the five years prior had spent over $70 million on infrastructure and upgrading. This puts it at the top end of organizational investment in information technologies (both for publicly and privately financed organizations).

So, in summary, the IMF was ideal for our research for two reasons. First, it is knowledge-centered and document-intensive; and second, its staff members have all the technologies they could want to support their work. What we wanted to find out was what role paper played in such an environment.

To answer these questions required us to develop an innovative set of methods. Without going into detail, suffice it to say that we relied on a mix of ethnography and a set of techniques that allowed us to measure and quantify behavior in the way a psychologist or an engineer would do.[4]

Ethnography is akin to studying a tribe in the wild. The ethnographer lives with the tribe, talks with the tribe, and (depending on one's school of thought) may even participate in the day-to-day activities of the tribe. The aim of ethnographers is to unpack and understand issues of culture and values, and the broader organizational or societal effects. Here, the IMF's staff (and mainly the economists) became the tribe of interest, studied in its natural habitat. It involved one of us working within the IMF over a period of six months, watching its key processes, including participating in IMF visits to governments abroad and interviewing over one hundred staff members (over ninety of them primarily knowledge workers). Our aim in this case was to try to understand what was important to those workers and how it was done. In particular, we were interested in issues of culture in relation to the documents and work practices they engaged in, to understand what they did and did not value, and to explore the ways in which their work practices affected and were influenced by larger social and organizational issues.

We combined this with methods that allowed us to record and quantify patterns of document use across different activities for a selected group of IMF staff. This level of description was focused on what the people we were studying *did* rather than on what they *said*. In other words, here we were interested in such issues as, How much of their time did they spend using paper versus digital technologies during the course of the day? For which kinds of activities did they tend to rely more on paper (or on digital tools)? How did activities differ across different groups of people? In order to look at these aspects we chose to use a diary study.

The diary study involved asking twenty-five people to keep a log of their daily activities over the course of five consecutive working days.[5] Of these twenty-five people, sixteen were professional knowledge workers (economists at various levels of seniority), seven were administrative assistants, and two were research assistants. Every day of the study, we asked each member of staff to make notes about the work activities they were engaged in and the approximate duration of those activities. At the end of the day, we used those notes to carry out a follow-up interview where we could clarify issues and note down more details about what they did. In this way, we were able to obtain fairly detailed and comprehensive information about a representative "slice" of the working processes of these twenty-five people. This also provided us with some quantitative data about the range of activities that these knowledge workers carried out with paper.

Paper Everywhere

When we began to analyze the data we had collected, we were somewhat surprised at the degree to which paper figured in the work. In our sample of twenty-five people we found 97 percent of their time was spent on activities that involved documents of some sort. Of this, 86 percent was spent on activities involving paper. However, a large proportion of that time, paper was used in combination with digital document tools, as shown in figure 3.1.

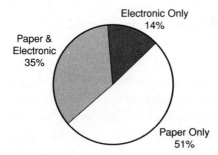

Figure 3.1
The degree to which paper and electronic tools were used in the document activities of twenty-five IMF staff members.

We further found that these sorts of numbers were not especially different for knowledge workers and for administrative workers. Both groups were using documents in almost all their work activities, with administrative staff using paper on average a somewhat higher percentage of the time. (For administrative staff, 89 percent of document-related activities involved paper, as compared to 81 percent for knowledge workers.) The breakdown with regard to the mix of paper only, paper and electronic, and electronic only was also very similar across these groups.

We began to try to classify the activities that people had recorded in their diaries and to map these onto the media used to support those activities. When we did this, differences between the groups soon began to emerge.

Figure 3.2 shows the activity profile for eight knowledge workers.[6] The profile shows that a large proportion of their time was spent on authoring activities, as one might expect. The chart also shows the extent to which these processes relied on paper. In particular, collaborative authoring processes, either in co-authoring a document or in reviewing the documents of others, were heavily paper-based. Paper was also often present in the drafting and editing of text and data, although this tended to be in conjunction with online tools.

We can also see from figure 3.2 that over half of conversations and the majority of meetings were supported by paper documents. Paper also tended to be the preferred medium for reading documents, for document delivery, for thinking and planning activities, and for document organization.

By comparison, figure 3.3 shows the activity profile for administrative tasks. While also heavily paper-based, by contrast the most frequent paper-based administrative activities were

- Referring to paper documents while entering or editing electronic text
- Organizing documents (e.g., filing and collating documents)
- Photocopying for distribution or filing purposes
- Sorting and distributing the mail
- Form filling
- Document delivery

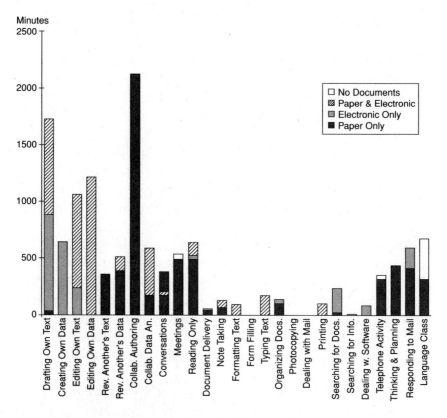

Figure 3.2
The activity profile for eight knowledge workers (professional economists).

From these simple statistics we begin to form a picture of the key roles of paper in the five-day window during which these members of staff kept diaries. We also begin to see the diversity of roles that paper played depending on the job of an individual.

What this shows is that while both knowledge workers and administrative staff members relied heavily on paper, it was for very different reasons. Knowledge workers were mainly using paper in their authoring activities: in the merging, reviewing, reading, and comparing of documents, and in the social processes surrounding the collaborative authoring of documents.

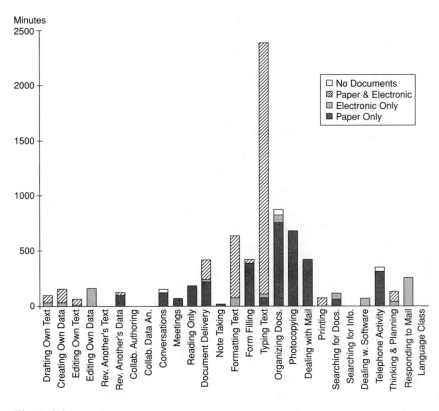

Figure 3.3
The activity profile for five administrative staff members.

Administrative assistants were largely involved in transforming paper-based text into electronic form and in the organization and dissemination of information. As it turns out, partly this was because paper was the medium in which the people they supported (the knowledge workers) delivered the information to them in the first place. It was also the medium in which these knowledge workers preferred that information be given back to them, for various reasons we discuss later.

It therefore seemed to us that key to understanding the ubiquity of paper in this organization was understanding how and why the knowledge workers were using it. The facts and figures coming from the diary data alone clearly did not tell the whole story. It only pointed to issues that the ethnographic data helped us to unravel and elaborate upon.

Paper in Knowledge Work

Authoring Work

As we have already begun to describe, the knowledge workers we studied spent a great deal of their time reading and writing, and meeting for the purpose of reading and writing. The ways in which paper supported these authoring activities can be understood by looking more closely at the nature of this work.

For example, one interesting result from the diary data was the high proportion of time that knowledge workers spent revising and reviewing reports (either their own or someone else's) as against actually drafting text, tables, and charts (71 percent versus 29 percent of their authoring activities). In other words, much of what they did was to spend time tinkering with or tweaking the documents before them.

One aspect of this has to do with the fact that almost all major reports that these knowledge workers dealt with were co-authored. This means that much of the authoring work was concerned with the integration of subsections of reports created by different people. In other words, a great deal of the work was involved in making sure the resulting report was much more than the sum of its individual parts. When the constituent parts of a report were brought together (such as different chapters and tables for a staff report), there was often a need for extensive negotiation and reiteration of that report's subsections. It was vitally important that the content of each section of a report be checked and iterated with reference to the larger report.

One reason this integration was a labor-intensive process was that the subsections that the IMF's knowledge workers produced involved significant degrees of professional judgment. As such, these judgments had to maintain consistency with the judgments of other people so that any single report presented a commonly agreed set of interpretations. Although extensive redrafting and review occurred with individual sections of reports, it often occurred at the point when authors started to integrate the subsections of their reports. In other words, the key finding here was that the work of integration of reports at the IMF was far more than a simple clerical process. In fact, it constituted an important part of the work of authoring.

In terms of actually modifying and editing sections of a report, knowledge workers mainly did this online. But, as we commonly observed, and as the diary data reflected, paper was nearly always used in conjunction with online editing (89 percent of the time). Knowledge workers would usually have many reports (such as other subsections of the same report or previous drafts) spread out around their computers when they were getting down to the job of editing. Numbers in graphs and spreadsheets had to be checked for consistency and accuracy, text had to be consulted to ensure consistency of content, style, and format, and old marked-up versions of reports had to be used to update online copies.

Paper supported these concurrent reading and writing activities so well because it could be spread out on the desktop, making the reports quickly and easily accessible. Further, these materials could be easily moved into the center of a desk, set alongside other pieces of paper, and flexibly organized and reorganized. While desk space was limited, it was not nearly as constraining as the screen of a workstation. Knowledge workers did use multiple windows on their computer screens, but this was mainly for electronic cutting and pasting, not for the back-and-forth cross-referencing of other materials during their authoring work.

Reviewing the Work of Others

Another important activity for the knowledge workers was reviewing other people's reports. Again, we found this was almost entirely a paper-based process. Occasionally knowledge workers reviewed their colleagues' spreadsheet data electronically, but even here this was always done in conjunction with paper. The papercentric nature of review existed despite the fact that the IMF's computer infrastructure and software applications supported both the delivery of the reports involved (including the spreadsheets) and the ability to make comments through a form of electronic Post-it notes.

There were two main sets of reasons for this. One set of reasons can be best captured with quotes from two knowledge workers whose main job was to review (rather than author) reports: "This is not the kind of work you can do on screen even if we got all the draft reports electronically.

You've got to print it out to do it properly. You have to settle down behind your desk and get into it."

In other words, having to read a report required hard copy. But this was not because of ease of reading and all that implies about screen resolution, viewing angle, and so on. What this individual had in mind was the need to settle down, to get "into" a report. Something about paper helped this.

As the other worker said, "I like to mark them up. You know I make all sorts of jottings on them."

In this case, to effectively analyze, comprehend, and review required the knowledge workers to mark up the report in question as well as to read it in paper form. In both cases, the individuals were pointing toward the need to bring to bear both the hands and the mind in intensive document activities.

Another set of issues had to do with how the marking up of a report preserved the distinction between a reviewer's comments and the original text. This was true in two senses. In one sense the distinction was a functional separation between suggested modifications and actual modifications. In other words, by marking on paper, actually implementing the changes was left to the discretion of the author and owner of the report. Comments on paper thus respected both the ownership and the accountability of the person who produced the report. It was not the job of the reviewer to make the changes. Only the author could do that, and only the author was held accountable for the end product. In another sense the distinction was perceptual. As handwriting on top of typed text, it was easy to perceive a reviewer's comments as distinct from the underlying text, so that areas where changes were suggested could be seen at a glance.

This last issue points to the fact that the ability to mark up text on paper provided a richness of representation that the electronic systems at the IMF did not support. For example, in cases where the same document might be reviewed by more than one person, the identity of the reviewer was indicated by the nature of the markings. Ideas could also be conveyed in a variety of ways by adding text, graphics, and sketches of tables, for example. Proofreading symbols were also used to show the ways in which text might be moved, deleted, or otherwise modified. This kind of markup language provided much more flexibility for annotation than the online Post-it notes did. We should also say that this online package was not vastly different from those available today.

Thinking, Planning, and Document Organization

Paper was also found to play an important role in what might best be described as thinking and planning activities, and in the organization of reports. Here, our observations are very similar to those of Alison Kidd,[7] who studied a range of different kinds of knowledge workers, including those in law, finance, advertising, and design.

Kidd found that knowledge workers rarely store and file paper documents or refer back to the information they do keep. Rather, it is the *process* of taking notes that is important in helping them to construct and organize their thoughts. The information that they do keep is arranged around their offices in a temporary holding pattern of paper documents that serves as a way of keeping available the inputs and ideas they might have use for in their current projects. This clutter also provides important contextual cues to remind them of where they were in their space of ideas. This study argues for the importance of the physicality of paper as the tangible embodiment of ideas and information.

At the IMF we also saw that the ease with which paper could be laid out in three-dimensional space, combined with the fact that paper rendered information tangible, made it indispensable for helping economists to keep ideas immediately available and accessible. The laying out of paper reports helped these knowledge workers to organize and structure their work, to remind them of what they needed to do, to keep available their current projects, and to allow immediate access to those ideas. They also spent time bringing together and organizing reports for themselves or other people in preparation for trips abroad, for example. In doing so, the accessibility and portability of these materials in paper form was an important factor, as was the act of flicking through these documents, bringing to mind what was in them and why they were important. The main implication of all this is that paper is important because it makes information accessible and tangible and gives it a persistent presence.

Collaborative Work

Another feature of the authoring process that emerged was the degree to which knowledge workers met face-to-face to discuss and co-author reports. We have described the ways in which economists edited and reviewed their own and others' work by themselves. But figure 3.4 shows the degree to which report editing and review was also collaborative. Specifically, we found that nearly half (44 percent) of these activities was carried out in face-to-face meetings.

As figure 3.4 shows, we found that this collaborative review process was especially reliant on use of paper. It was involved with paper 82 percent of the time, the other 18 percent of the time involving online tools in conjunction with the use of paper reports.

How this collaborative authoring works is further illustrated by looking in more detail at the process over time. Figure 3.5 shows a picture of the

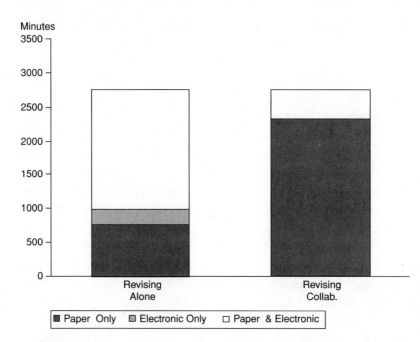

Figure 3.4
Time spent revising and editing both alone and with other people as a function of different media.

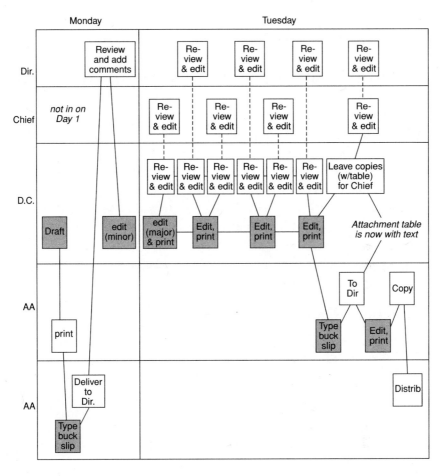

Figure 3.5
Two days of data from the daily activities of five people involved in the production
of a report: three knowledge workers (a director, a chief, and a deputy chief), and
two administrative assistants. White boxes refer to activities mainly involving
paper; shaded boxes refer to activities mainly involving online tools. The order of
activities is represented along the horizontal axis. Dotted vertical lines indicate
face-to-face meetings.

flow of activities for the creation and review of a note for the IMF's management, its executive board, taken from our daily activity logs. This case involved three economists (of various levels of seniority) and two administrative assistants. Note that while much of the drafting and editing of the text was done online by one individual alone, there was extensive editing and review of the report on paper and in meetings with the other two. This process was iterative, involving several collaborative review sessions interspersed with online editing and then printing.

Our research confirmed that the same process of collaboration held true of many other types of reports, such as reports that underwent formal review processes. For here, although the reviewing team would spend some time going over the report on their own, a key event was to meet and discuss their interpretations together. Again, paper was essential to these collaborative review processes, invariably involving the collaborative marking up and reading of one or more paper-based reports.

Paper was essential to these collaborative processes because it supported what one might call the "social mechanisms" that occurred during these activities. One aspect of paper that made it important for face-to-face discussions was its physicality. Because paper is a physical embodiment of information, actions performed in relation to paper are, to a large extent, made visible to one's colleagues. Reviewers sitting around a desk could tell whether a colleague was turning toward or away from a report; whether she was flicking through it or setting it aside. Contrast this with watching someone across a desk looking at a document on a laptop. What are they looking at? Where in the document are they? Are they really reading their e-mail? Knowing these things is important because they help a group coordinate its discussions and reach a shared understanding of what is being discussed. These issues are further discussed in chapter 5.

A second aspect was that, with paper, discussion could be easily carried on in parallel with marking up and examining parts of a report. Because paper is easily shared and quick to access, colleagues could manipulate the pages so that the relevant ones (for the topic of the discussion) could be placed side-by-side and dealt with; they could annotate the relevant sections as the discussions were under way. Doing these things did not require a great deal of attention to distract from and disrupt the discussions.

Rather, the documents in question did quite the reverse: they provided a focus for the talking and helped the discussions move along.[8]

This can be contrasted with the word-processing applications and computers available at the IMF. Though these were state-of-the-art, they made it more difficult to do these things. If a document needed to be modified, doing so would require everyone but the owner of the computer to wait while the relevant data entry was undertaken. Moving between pages with the scroll bar would be tiresome for all concerned (not just the person at the computer). Once they got to the right place in the document, people had to watch while "more fiddling" would take place, as one person put it. To be sure, such systems enabled changes to the master document to be made in meetings, but it was disruptive to the central process at hand, namely, the talking.

Delivery of Reports

A fifth and final activity in which paper appeared to play a key role was in the delivery of reports. By key role we do not mean here that hand delivery of paper was a very frequent activity but rather that when it occurred, the activity itself was perceived to be an important and significant event.

At the IMF, once a major report has been completed, it was delivered to various individuals for review (or more precisely, individuals representing various departments). When we looked closely at the nature of report delivery within the IMF, it became clear that there were important issues to do with the process of handing over reports between the authors and reviewers. Although automatic routing was part of current practice, on many occasions authors of reports wanted to be involved at the point of delivery. To ensure this, they opted to hand-deliver paper documents to reviewers. When we spoke to them, it became clear there were good reasons for this:

• *Documents don't always speak for themselves.*   Discussion could add value to the report at the point of delivery. There were many things that could be discussed, such as how much time the review was likely to take, the issues that were unusual in the particular report, the general context of the report, and so on. These related to the need for extensive discussions surrounding reports already remarked upon.

• *Showing deference.*   There were issues to do with what one might loosely describe as the culture of the IMF. Some individuals said they preferred to deliver reports by hand to reflect the importance of the report in question. As one individual put it, "Delivering papers (for review) is too important to leave to e-mail."

• *Personalizing relationships.*   Hand delivery enabled authors to personalize their relations with reviewers. This may be important when, organizationally speaking, reviewers may be in a potentially antagonistic position vis-à-vis authors. By delivering a document, authoring staff were helping to smooth and oil that relationship, not so much to bypass the concerns of reviewers as to make elicitation of those concerns something that could be done more easily. In other words, hand delivery humanized and personalized these processes. Paper provided the context for such behavior.

• *Making sure it gets there.*   A fourth and final point relates not just to delivery of reports to reviewers but to the delivery of documents in general. As many members of the IMF mentioned when interviewed, delivery of a paper document was a way of "making sure it gets there." Because it was a physical manifestation of a document, handing it over not only confirmed delivery; its physical presence on someone's desk drew attention to itself and served as a continual reminder to the recipient that action needed to be taken.

Knowledge Work Beyond the IMF

We have talked about many ways, then, that paper supported the work of the IMF's knowledge workers. We might well ask at this point, How typical are these findings? Isn't the IMF a very unusual place? In some ways, the answer to this is definitely yes. The IMF is indeed a unique environment, and its workers have a special set of skills. But we have found that in other ways, the answer is no. We have found that these knowledge workers showed us ways in which paper supported their work in much the same way that it supports knowledge work in many other diverse kinds of settings. Since looking at the IMF, we have looked at many other workplaces: hospitals, telecommunications companies, manufacturers, design companies, and many more. So far, we have yet to see a place where paper does not figure in these same kinds of activities.

However, we were concerned about generalizing too much. We wanted to find out more about how typical the IMF is in terms of the activities of its workers, the technological competence of the organization, and their reliance on documents.

We began by comparing our quantitative analyses of the activities of knowledge workers and administrative staff to other analyses that cut across different organizations. There have been a number of such analyses over the years.[9] However, it is often difficult to make comparisons because there is a great deal of variation in the kinds of activity categories used and in the definitions of the different categories. In this case, a comparison between our own data and a large Booz-Allen & Hamilton study cutting across a number of organizations[10] allowed the best (although rough) comparison, the results of which are shown in figure 3.6.[11]

Figure 3.6 shows that with the exception of the proportion of time spent in meetings and in analyzing material, the numbers are quite similar. This was especially striking considering that our numbers came from a relatively

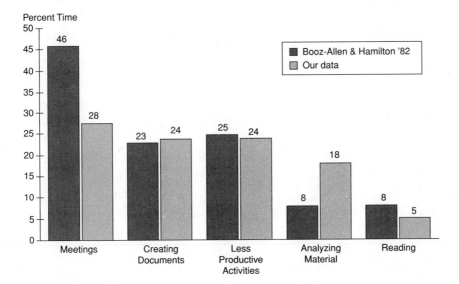

Figure 3.6
A comparison of the data from the activity analysis of IMF knowledge workers with that of a large 1982 study by Booz-Allen & Hamilton (cited in H. Poppel, "Who Needs the Office of the Future?").

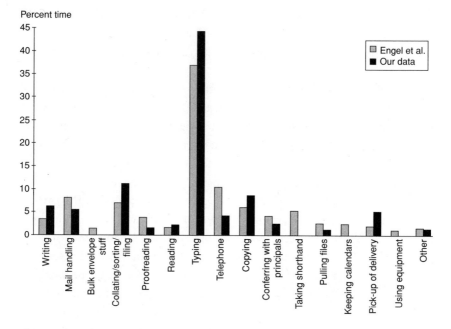

Percent time

Figure 3.7
A comparison of the data from the activity analysis of IMF administrative assistants with that of a 1979 study by Engel et al. (cited in R. A. Hirscheim, *Office Automation*).

small sample of workers (eight), albeit over the course of five consecutive days. The similarity was especially interesting given that our study and theirs are thirteen years apart.

With regard to the data on administrative staff, our best basis of comparison came from a study done in 1979, which offers a breakdown of the amount of time secretaries spend on various activities.[12] Again, because of difficulties in matching the categories, it offers only a rough comparison (figure 3.7).[13] It does show, however, that the kinds of activities done by administrative staff then and now do not appear to be vastly different. Even with a gap of about twenty years, typing (or in today's terms, word processing) still appears to be the main activity of administrative assistants. In fact, in terms of relative proportions, four of the top five activities for each of the studies are the same: typing, collating/sorting/filing, mail handling, and photocopying.

These very rough comparisons gave us some basis for believing that the activities of both knowledge workers and administrative assistants at the IMF were not atypical. Further, when one considers that these comparisons were made with data collected between one or two decades ago, it appears that there is also considerable stability over time.

Of course, one interpretation might be that the similarity of the IMF results to such outdated data reflects the fact that the IMF is itself behind the times with regard to its technological tools and practices. But as we noted earlier, the IMF was and is technologically progressive. Although it is a publicly financed institution and hence might be thought of as being undercapitalized, in fact its per capita investment figures puts the IMF at the top end of banking and financial institution investment levels.

If the activities at the IMF seem to be very similar to many other organizations, what about its heavy reliance on documents? Unfortunately, other studies don't tell us much about this. But we do know from the work of other researchers that a vast range of different kinds of work revolve around and rely on documents, from government workers to software engineers to designers.[14] The likelihood is that the document-centered nature of the IMF is far from unusual and indeed may be the norm in many knowledge-intensive organizations. Indeed, the term *knowledge worker* may in itself be very misleading. Attaching this sort of formal label (i.e., whether an individual is labeled as a professional or not) may not be the way to look at whether knowledge-based work characterizes an organization. For example, a study of telephone operators[15] has shown that even the most clerical and apparently routine activities involve a significant knowledge work component. This suggests it may be more sensible to ask to what degree different kinds of work involve this component. To the degree that they do, we might expect paper to play a role in the ways we have mapped out in this chapter.

Conclusion

Like many organizations, the IMF has over the years introduced a variety of networked electronic document tools only to discover that paper remains an important medium in work. What we discovered is that there were complex reasons for the persistence of paper, the most significant of which is that paper serves the IMF's knowledge workers well for the tasks they have to hand. These individuals use paper at certain stages in their work not because they are unwilling to change, but because the technology they are provided with as an alternative to paper does not offer all they need. As a result, they continue to use paper because its functionalities support important aspects of their work. These functionalities or, if you will, these affordances of paper, are related both to interactional issues—how users deal with documents in their hands and on their desktops—and to more broad organizational and culture factors such as the need to show deference to reviewing departments, and so on.

Since the time of our study we have noticed that when we look at most workplaces, it is easy to see who is engaged in intensive knowledge work: it is the person whose desk is strewn with paper. Find a desk littered with stacks of reports, written notes, and every inch of space used up, and you will find someone creating a document, planning work, or doing some other sort of deeply reflective activity. This is as true of "old-fashioned" workplaces as it is of the most high-tech environments. We have seen it at the IMF, and we have seen it in so-called paperless offices.

All this is not to say that new technologies have no place in knowledge work. Indeed, at the IMF and elsewhere, technology is ubiquitous and heavily deployed. But this has not resulted in paper's disappearing. More often than not it has resulted in the use of both paper and digital media in combination. The place of paper on the desktop is very likely to be next to or surrounding the desktop computer. In our briefcases when we travel, for example, we are as likely to carry an array of digital tools (mobile phone, digital organizer, and portable computer) as we are to carry paper. And the plethora of printers and scanners in the workplace are testament to our need in today's modern knowledge workplaces to convert the digital into paper form as well as to convert from paper documents back to digital form.

In chapter 4 we report more research that looks more deeply at the use of paper in reading. Reading was an activity embedded in most of the things that the IMF knowledge workers did but hardly ever talked about as just "reading." It was a part of authoring and reviewing and all the other more complex activities we described in this chapter. In chapter 5 we look at the role paper plays in collaborative and team situations. Here the situation is, in some ways, more complex than in the case of reading, because many forms of collaborative work practices have developed hand-in-hand with paper-based documentation. This has resulted in an intimate relationship between the affordances of paper and organizational processes. In these situations the role of paper can be altered, but that also requires change in the processes. When we have looked at both reading and collaborative work in more detail, we will be in a better position to judge the importance of paper to knowledge work and to discuss the possibility of whether technological alternatives can ever supplant paper in the kinds of activities we have highlighted at the IMF.

4

Reading from Paper

As we mentioned in chapter 1, the myth of the paperless office has been perpetuated over the years by a series of technological developments, most notably the desktop computer and the Internet. More recently, renewed excitement has been fueled by developments that promise to support our ability to read digital documents as easily as we can read from paper. These include advances in wireless networking, battery, and display technologies resulting in digital display devices that are now more mobile and interactive than ever. New products include the first e-book devices (portable electronic devices designed specifically to support reading). Alongside this, the merging of big media publishing organizations with technology and service providers has promised to make vast repositories of digital content available to consumers. Virtual bookshops are now selling specially formatted electronic versions of books, e-book standards are being developed, and some companies are even developing special fonts aimed at making electronic reading easier on the eyes.

As a result of all this, many technologists believe that we are on the verge of solving what they see as one of the last great obstacles to realizing a paperless future, namely, the problem of reading from screens instead of paper. This has led to the latest predictions of doom for paper: the death of the book is now imminent. Indeed, so excited are some by the prospect of there no longer being a need for bound paper books that there is talk of bookless libraries. According to this vision, there will be no need for physical libraries full of paper. Instead, people can seek out and have delivered over networks to their desktops or portable computers the contents of any book, journal, newspaper, or magazine. Similarly, the future of publishing is seen as one that will undergo huge changes in the digital age. We are already seeing publishing move away from preordained print runs to a situation where books are only printed on demand. It is not much of a conceptual leap to then foresee not only the end of the library as we know it but also the end of the bookshop as we know it. It is also no stretch of the imagination to predict that we can do away with printing for reading altogether. After all, if readers have the text they want displayed on their digital devices, why bother to print at all?

These hopes have a great deal to recommend them. The idea of overcoming barriers of time and space, and to have available at one's fingertips huge stores of electronic text to search through and access at any time, in any place is very appealing. Yet at the same time there is something curious about them. We have only to think about what most of us do to know that when it comes to reading, we prefer paper. Certainly, we may use electronic means to create or seek out documents. Equally, we may use our computers to receive and send documents to others. But when it comes to settling down and reading something (especially a long or important document) we often print it before we read it. Why is this? Is it simply that the technology isn't quite there yet, or is something else going on?

The Affordances of Paper for Reading

One reason most of us can point to is that we don't like to read from computer screens. We complain about the poor visibility of text on screens, the feeling of tired eyes when reading large quantities of text online, and issues such as screen flicker, poor resolution, and so on. However, our dislike of text on computer screens is only a small part of the puzzle. Why we *like* paper for reading is in some ways more interesting. In the course of our own explorations we have found there are four main reasons why paper supports reading so successfully:

1. Paper helps us flexibly navigate through documents.
2. Paper facilitates the cross-referencing of more than one document at a time.
3. Paper allows us to annotate documents easily.
4. Paper allows the interweaving of reading and writing.

These facts about reading are still not generally recognized as the major differences between the paper and the digital worlds when it comes to reading. Those scientifically studying reading have typically looked at other issues that have led them away from these matters and focused mainly on issues to do with comparing the readability of text presented on a computer screen to text on paper. At the same time, those who design and develop technologies of reading have often been more interested in getting the best performance from their hardware and software than in properly understanding what reading involves.

It is perhaps no surprise, then, that the technologies that have been developed to support reading to date have not been as successful as predicted. Unfortunately, most technologies about to enter the marketplace seem to be based on a similarly poor understanding and are therefore fated to have an equally bad reception. This is not to say that electronic alternatives to paper are without a role when it comes to reading. (Indeed, as we explore in chapter 6, by taking these properties into account we believe it *is* possible to build better electronic alternatives.) But it is to say that there are things that people do when they read on paper that have not been properly considered by those who design new technology. If they had been considered, then e-books, document-reading devices, and other electronic alternatives to paper would be better suited to support the tasks set them.

In this chapter we tell the story of how we came to these conclusions. Until recently, researchers didn't look at what was going on when people read in day-to-day situations. Instead, they set up experiments where the focus was on such things as how easy it is to read words on a screen versus reading words on paper.[1] In so doing, they missed important issues, such as how and why people read documents in the real world. This is nearly always bound up with whether people are at work or at home, what jobs they have, and the reasons they are reading. If these researchers had based their studies more closely on what happens in real settings, they would have seen that it isn't simply a matter of the speed with which the eyes and brain can perceive and comprehend the meaning of words. Similarly, it isn't simply a matter of the amount of fatigue or strain the eyes experience during the course of reading.

Our own alternative approach to looking at reading took us to settings as diverse as hospitals, lawyers' offices, airports, and financial institutions.

This led us to uncover many interesting facts about how people do reading in their work. For example, there are different types of reading in different work settings. Some people, such as doctors and nurses, read as part of the process of filling out forms. Other people have jobs that require them to read documents that they then have to discuss, such as lawyers and marketing managers. Still others have jobs that entail spending considerable time cross-referencing documents. For example, pilots have to make sure that flight plans correspond to one another, and accountants check that figures are consistent across different tables and forms.

By understanding the nature of the reading tasks people really do, we were then in a position to carry out some of our research in a laboratory to focus on these kinds of tasks. Only then could we look in more detail at the properties of paper and electronic document media that are important when people read. Here we were particularly interested in why and how people annotate documents, why they make notes or write on one document while reading another, and how, in various ways, readers attempt to make sense of the text in front of them by navigating through documents and spreading paper out around them. These issues are more or less typical of the reading activities we have observed in the real world. All this led us to discover the affordances of paper that make it useful for reading.

Reading in the Real World

To begin, then, we and some of our colleagues from Xerox PARC wanted to look at reading activities not only in depth but also in terms of their breadth and diversity. We wanted to understand the richness of those activities and the ways in which reading is embedded within broader contexts. Reading, especially in the workplace, is never undertaken by itself. We wanted to understand not only how paper is used to support these activities but also how computers play a role and how paper and digital technologies may be used in conjunction with one another. Asking people to carry out predefined reading tasks within the confines of a research laboratory is not a good way to identify these sorts of issues in the first instance. Other techniques are better.

Here we drew heavily on our experience at the IMF. This taught us how commonplace are document-related tasks in the workplace as well as how ubiquitous paper can be. But it also indicated how great was the variation in work done with documents by people with different jobs. What was needed was a method that would indicate what these differences might be in a variety of settings. Here, as with the IMF, we chose to use a diary technique so that we could record the activities of people in their own work settings and in a range of professions.

A diary study involves asking a group of individuals to keep a daily log of their activities for a period of time. These activities can be almost anything. In our case we wanted a diary of activities that involved documents. Since we assumed the instances of such activities would be many, we asked for the diaries to be kept only for five consecutive working days by each person in the study. By "documents" we meant any sort of documents, whether paper-based documents like books and Post-it notes or electronic "documents" like computer-based documents and the use of beepers, pagers, and palm-tops. Hence each person logged any document activity, not just reading activities. At the end of each day, interviews were carried out using a structured form to expand on the description of each activity and to note down such things as what types of documents were used, whether the activity was collaborative, where the activity occurred, and what additional tools were used. This kind of diary keeping must be accompanied by regular and frequent interviews to fully understand the details of what people write down.

For the study we wanted a group whose jobs varied in at least three major ways:

1. *Mobility.*   We wanted people whose jobs were predictably mobile across several locations, some who were unpredictable in terms of location, and some who were centrally based in one location.

2. *Location.*   We wanted some people who worked across a variety of "activity locations," such as traditional offices, retail offices, home offices, and other work sites (e.g., cars, client sites, operating rooms).

3. *Collaboration.*   We wanted a sample of people who varied greatly in the extent to which their work habits involved collaboration with others,

and whose habits involved sharing and reading documents with other people to different degrees.

Taking all these factors into account led us to recruit a group of fifteen people comprising

- An airline pilot
- A general surgeon
- An organ transplant ward coordinator/nurse
- A residential architect
- A real estate agent
- Two lawyers (one senior and one more junior)
- Two anesthetists
- A warden of a halfway house
- An accounting assistant
- An optician
- A marketing manager
- An executive from a small startup company
- A social worker

The resulting group consisted of people with very different kinds of working habits. Some were highly mobile, such as the airline pilot, the marketing manager, and the startup executive. These people were frequently away from any sort of office at a variety of unpredictable locations: in the sky, on a train, or on the road. Others were more locally mobile within their working sites or at local client sites, such as the two anesthetists, the real estate agent, and the architect. Still others were mostly office-bound, such as the lawyers, the optician, and the accountant. These factors affected the kinds of technological infrastructure they had to hand and the kinds of devices and technologies they needed to carry with them.

The degree to which the work at these sites involved working with and sharing documents also varied tremendously. Some people worked as part of tightly organized teams, such as the surgeon and the nurse, who worked as part of an organ transplant ward. While their work was largely team-based, they rarely looked at or read documents together. Others worked together more loosely but nonetheless spent a great deal of time meeting with others for the express purpose of discussing documents with colleagues or clients. Both the marketing manager and the social worker fell into this category. In other cases, people worked independently of one another, and with their own documents, such as the accountant, the real estate agent, the warden, and the architect.

Studying this group of individuals thus seemed a promising way of beginning to understand the diversity of reading. Diaries were filled out, and interviews took anywhere from half an hour to three hours each evening. By the end of the study, we had over seventy days' worth of information about the work these people did, the documents and technologies they used, and the kinds of reading they engaged in. We classified and analyzed these findings in detail and, where possible, quantified the amount of time each person spent doing different kinds of reading (as well as writing) during the course of the work week.

The result was that we were to radically overhaul our notions of reading. We uncovered eight main findings.[2]

The Ubiquity of Reading

Most activities people do at work involve documents, and reading in some form or other occurs in most of these activities. We found that, on average, 82 percent of the activities carried out by our study group of fifteen people involved documents. Some kind of reading occurred in over 70 percent of these document-related activities, pointing both to its importance as well as its ubiquity.

The Preference for Paper

Paper is the medium of choice for reading, even when the most high-tech technologies are to hand. Despite the interesting differences in how people were reading in the various work settings we looked at, one thing all these people had in common was their reliance on paper for reading. When we analyzed the diaries, we found that paper-based reading and writing accounted for 85 percent of people's total document-related activity time. Online reading and writing made up only about 13 percent of that total time. (The remaining 2 percent involved reading from projected slides, which were classified separately.) These figures more or less confirmed the figures we had obtained from our study of the IMF. Moreover, as with the

IMF, these figures were especially interesting in light of the fact that all the people in our study had jobs that required them to use computers for at least some portion of their work. Nor were any of our group unfamiliar with technology or working in situations with low levels of technical and technological support.

Many Different Kinds of Reading

Reading takes on a range of forms, is done for a variety of purposes, and is associated with a diverse set of other activities. People skim through a document to get a feel for its contents; they carefully read another document so that they properly understand the issues (to "self-inform," as one of our subjects put it); they compare several reports when checking facts and figures. In fact, we identified ten categories of work-related reading (figure 4.1).

Different Ways of Reading

If we had had any conventional notions of what it means to read, we had to radically revise them when we looked at the kinds of reading that the people in our study did most frequently (figure 4.2). Reading was sometimes lightweight, involving quick glances, and at other times intensive and reflective. In work situations it was rare that people sat by themselves, started reading from the beginning of a document, and read through page by page to the end. Nor was reading sequential. Rather, more often it involved flicking through pages, place holding, navigating back and forth between different sections, and using indices or tables. Rarely was the reading continuous. More typically, it was interrupted or undertaken in short spurts. Finally, reading was not always undertaken alone. Often it occurred in group situations, where people jointly viewed or discussed documents.

Reading in Conjunction with Writing

Reading occurs with writing more often than it occurs without. This was one of the most striking of the findings. We found that in the diaries reading occurred in conjunction with some kind of writing activity over 75 percent of the time and up to 91 percent of the time. By writing we mean a

Reading to identify   Glancing at a document only in order to *identify* what a document is or what type of document it is.

Skimming   Reading rapidly in order to establish a rough idea of what is written, to decide whether any of its contents might be useful, or whether anything needs to be read in more detail later.

Reading to remind   Reading specifically in order to remind oneself of what to do next, e.g., a to-do list, shopping list, Post-it note.

Reading to search for answers to questions   Reading to search for particular information: to answer a question, for reference, or to obtain information necessary to make a decision. This kind of reading is goal-directed ranging from very simple goals to complex decision-making or problem-solving tasks.

Reading to self-inform   Reading for the purpose of furthering general knowledge without any specific goal to which the information will be applied.

Reading to learn   Reading with the goal of being able to relate or apply information at a later date. Includes reading to review the basic concepts for discussion, or reading which is much more reflective in nature.

Reading for cross-referencing   Reading across more than one document or more than one page in order to integrate information. This is often done for the purpose of writing, and may well include some editing activities.

Reading to edit or critically review text   Reading in order to monitor what has been written in terms of content, style, grammar, syntax, and/or overall presentation. Includes editing one's own text, seeing how one's own text fits into a collaborative document, or the review of the text of others.

Reading to support listening   Reading in order to support listening to someone else talk (e.g., following a presentation by looking at a series of slides).

Reading to support discussion   Referring to a document during a discussion in order to establish a mutual frame of reference and focus for discussion. Usually takes place in a face-to-face meeting.

Figure 4.1
A taxonomy of work-related reading.

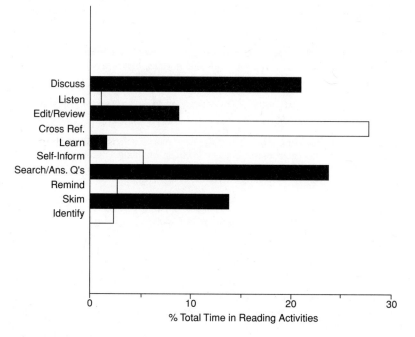

Figure 4.2
Frequency of reading categories averaged across fifteen people.

range of activities involving making marks on paper or on computer screens. We mean notetaking, annotation (writing on top of existing text), form filling, and creating or modifying new documents. These activities, whether they were done on paper or on a computer, tended to be interwoven with the reading process.

Use of Multiple Documents

Reading involves multiple documents as often as it involves one document at a time. During the course of our interviews we were struck by the fact that many of the reading activities people undertook were not confined to single pieces of paper or to single computer screens but involved reading across several pieces of paper, or reading across a piece of paper and a computer. When we looked at this more closely, we found that in terms of time spent in different reading activities, only about half of the time did the reading rely on a single display surface (single piece of paper or single computer screen). The other half of the time these readers were using at least two display surfaces concurrently (and sometimes many more than two). They spread out pages side-by-side, over desks, and onto floors. They often used paper next to a computer screen, or sometimes in conjunction with more than one computer screen (see figure 4.3). Sometimes it was clear that these activities involved reading from one screen or piece of paper while writing on another; sometimes no writing was involved at all; rather the reading activity itself was taking place across more than one screen or page.

There were four main reasons our readers did this:

1. *Extracting information.* Some people wanted to extract information, for the purpose of filling out forms, for example. This involved searching for the information in one document, taking notes, and transforming the information to include in another document. Often, a separate piece of paper was used as a computational workspace for manipulating figures drawn from other documents, or for writing summaries or plans of action.

Figure 4.3
Reading across multiple documents, both paper and electronic, with pen in hand.

2. *Integrating information.* On other occasions, people wanted to integrate various bits of information from diverse sources to create something new or to make decisions about an issue. This involved reading across at least two and sometimes more documents for specific facts and figures, or for general ideas and themes. Other instances involved integrating information for the purpose of making some kind of decision by considering information from different places. Or, people would literally integrate information across documents, such as updating one document using another (e.g., incorporating paper-based changes into an electronic version of a document, or using old to-do lists to create new ones).

3. *Checking for consistency.* Another reason people referred to more than one document at the same time was to check information, such as facts, figures, language, or format, for consistency across documents. This often involved flicking back and forth between the documents.

4. *Critiquing or making comments.* People carried out integrated reading and writing activities when they were critiquing or reviewing something, or referring to one document in order to write another, such as writing a letter in response to one received.

The Complex Role of Technology
All these more general findings to some extent belie the actual complexity of the activities that our participants recorded and told us about. Reading is best understood as part of an intricate set of activities bound up with the technologies to hand. We can illustrate this with a "day in the life" scenario (figure 4.4) taken from one of the participants of our diary study, who was an executive for a startup company.[3] It shows how the reading activities of this person changed throughout the day and depended on where he was, what he was trying to accomplish, and whom he was with. Some of the reading activities were quite short and interwoven with jottings or online writing. Others were more prolonged and involved several kinds of reading from browsing to proofreading to reviewing. Throughout, the activities, all tied to his job, were accomplished with a variety of digital technologies supported by paper.

When we compare diary descriptions of the airline pilot, surgeon, or real estate agent, they of course look very different. However, they have in

A Day in the Life of JA

JA travels frequently and has a busy home life as well as working life. He has his own startup company but is helping to get two others off the ground. Working both from his car and his home office, he has to handle technology that includes two computers (a Mac and a PC), a fax machine, a printer, a telephone, a beeper, a cell phone, a scanner, and a zip drive. JA also often works at other people's offices and makes use of the local print shop to prepare and finish glossy documents for clients.

1. Reads newspapers (sometimes tears out articles, points of interest).
2. Receives message on beeper at home; returns call to startup #2.
3. Receives message on beeper in car; returns call to startup #1 (talks about meeting preparation).
4. Senior staff meeting at CEO's house for startup #1 over breakfast. JA makes general notes on paper.
5. Home office: checks voicemail, writes out list of things on paper to follow up on, from various meetings since last there (including evening/phone meetings).
6. Reads and reviews several paper documents from colleagues as well as an outside agency (about public relations and business plans). JA edits them on paper, sends them to other reviewers via the fax machine, and uses one of the documents to compose his own document on the computer.
7. Drafts custom business plan another colleague has sent to him as an e-mail attachment. Does this on the computer while referring to some rough notes on paper.
8. Does a Web search for information related to laser surgery. Bookmarks the location and e-mails to request further information. Prints out the document to read later and to file in in-house library.
9. Faxes a memo to a colleague via the computer.
10. Checks and responds to e-mail.
11. Revises computerized to-do list using scribbled notes and printed out e-mail.
12. Fills out a paper purchase order form, which he then faxes.
13. Prepares corporate presentation: assembles a custom slide set from 35 mm slides and photocopies accompanying materials to hand out.
14. Give presentation at startup (1 hour), hands out hard copies, and takes notes throughout other people's presentations.
15. Does file backup at home using zip drive.

Figure 4.4
A day in the life of an executive for a startup company, focusing on his document-related activities.

common a diversity of activity and the use of paper and electronic technologies in support of each other.

Clusters of Readers

Even though there is great diversity in the kinds of reading people do on the job, there are also characteristic clusters that emerge. When we looked across our sample of fifteen people and considered their reading and writing activities, we found they could be clustered to some extent according to the main kinds of reading they did (see figure 4.1), the main kinds of writing they did (note taking, form filling, creating new documents, or annotating existing documents), and the degree to which viewing of documents tended to be shared with others (table 4.1).

Form Fillers   The document activities of all four medical personnel (surgeon, anesthetists, and nurse) were very much centered on paper form fill-

Table 4.1
Important Dimensions Related to Reading, and How They Varied Across Workers

Person	Most Frequent Reading Category	Most Frequent Writing Category	Shared Viewing Category
Architect	Edit/Review	Creation	Low
Pilot	Cross-reference	Note taking	Medium
Warden	Cross-reference	Form filling	Medium
Accounting assistant	Cross-reference	Form filling	Low
Lawyer (junior)	Cross-reference	Creation	Low
Lawyer (senior)	Discussion	Annotation	Medium
Optician	Discussion	Form filling	High
Social worker	Discussion	Note taking	High
Marketing manager	Discussion	Annotation	High
Startup executive	Discussion	Creation	Medium
Real estate agent	Search/Answer	Note taking	Low
Nurse	Search/Answer	Form filling	Low
Surgeon	Search/Answer	Form filling	Low
Anesthetist 1	Search/Answer	Form filling	Low
Anesthetist 2	Search/Answer	Form filling	Low

ing. Their main reading tasks consisted of searching through documents for facts, results, instructions, and other specific kinds of information in order to complete these forms. This kind of document activity was, in the main, something they did on their own (although the documents they interacted with were generally jointly authored).

Discussants   A second group of people spent a great deal of time reading in support of discussion. They read in preparation for discussions, read during and in support of discussions, and read documents produced as a result of discussions. This included the senior lawyer, the optician, the social worker, the marketing manager, and the startup executive. As one might expect, these people were in the "high" or "medium" shared-viewing category (see table 4.1).

Cross-Referencers   In the third group were those who spent considerable time reading across multiple documents. This included the accounting assistant, the pilot, the warden, and the junior lawyer. This activity was done for different reasons, however. The accounting assistant spent most of her time cross-referencing to check for consistency among figures in different documents; the pilot integrated and extracted from multiple documents to plan routes and check flight information; the warden mainly extracted information from multiple documents for form filling; and the junior lawyer cross-referenced to check the language and format of existing documents to help in the creation of new ones.

Summary
These, then, are the main features of work-related reading. By looking at reading in the real world rather than by trying to assume the properties of reading beforehand, we were able to determine many things that had not been recognized in existing research in any comprehensive way. It had not been recognized before how much time is given over to reading in the workplace, nor how often reading also involves annotation and writing. In addition, nowhere had it really been noted just how diverse are the kinds of tasks within which reading is embedded, with each particular task having its own constitutive features. When thinking about how to design reading

technologies, it is important to know that the reader who skims does one kind of task and the person who reads reflectively does another. This shows itself in the manner of reading: one person will flick through pages very rapidly, often moving back and forth, whereas the other will stop and focus on certain sections, usually with pen in hand. Neither will necessarily read a report or document from beginning to end; indeed, the idea that documents are mostly read in such a fashion, at least in work situations, is wholly wrong.

As we discuss in chapter 6, these findings (in terms of what people do in common and how they vary) have important implications for the design of devices to support reading. To better understand what the specific features of those designs might be, however, required us to look more closely at how different kinds of reading are carried out. This called for a look at reading in a laboratory setting, where the specific ways in which people interact with paper versus computer screens while reading can be studied in all their rich detail.

How Paper Supports Reading

The advantage of having first looked at reading in the real world was that we were able to design a laboratory study that we could be sure would be representative of the kinds of activities that people typically do when they read. Obviously, it would not be possible to investigate in an experimental way every aspect of reading (after all, the very point of experimental research is to be selective and economical). But our investigations had indicated that three issues were important.

First, one of the most striking of our findings was how often reading is done with pen in hand, or it is done when a computer is also used to support writing. It seemed appropriate, therefore, that any task we chose should require reading with writing. Second, many reading activities involved working with more than one document at a time. This therefore had to be a feature of the study. Third, given the variety of ways in which people read, we wanted a task that would involve as many different kinds of reading as we could incorporate, ranging from skimming to reflective reading.

In light of this, we chose a task that involved reading and summarizing. This was interesting because it required the interweaving of reading and writing; it required more than one document; and it required a mix of reading activities, including quick search and navigation as well as a deep understanding of the document being summarized. It also had the benefit of being a task that people did not find too unnatural or artificial.

We set up a study in which we aimed to obtain detailed descriptions of people's reading behavior when asked to summarize a general science article.[4] Ten people took part: five using only paper and pen, and five using only online tools on a PC. Other than these constraints, they were free to do anything they wanted to get the task done. Each session was video-recorded. On completion, we asked the participants questions about their activities during the task. In addition, they were shown, and asked to comment on, various video clips of their behavior that we had noted as being interesting. These clips helped to cue people's memories as to what they had been doing and why.

The Need for Flexible Navigation

The study showed that both paper and online readers spent a good deal of time moving or navigating through their documents. In the task we asked them to do, this navigation served at least three important functions: planning, checking facts, and checking understanding.

Both the paper and online readers talked about the need to make connections between different parts of a document to get an overall sense of its structure as well as to create a plan for writing about what was in it. This was supported by skimming through the text:

Interviewer: This bit is where you seem to flick through some pages.

Paper Reader: I get the first and second pages and then look at the third. . . . [I'm] trying to connect bits of information to write on my plan—areas that I want included in the same paragraph—or topics I want included in my paragraph.

Readers were also seen scanning the science article to check on facts, particular expressions, and spellings:

Online Reader: I was looking for the 'dragon's blood tree.' I was trying to find that name. . . . I couldn't remember exactly what they called it.

Finally, moving through the document helped readers to check their understanding of the text. There were several times when readers needed to re-read sections of the document to confirm or clarify their understanding:

Interviewer: You refer back to it after you have read something up here.

Paper Reader: Yes, it was because of the name of the tree—Cinnabar. And I needed to know if it was the same tree as they talked about over here.

There were, however, considerable differences in the ease with which these sorts of navigational tasks could be carried out on paper versus online. The videotapes illustrated the speed and skill with which paper readers were able to move through the documents we gave them. Here, we saw readers begin to turn pages well before they were finished reading them. Such anticipatory actions are characteristic of highly skilled activity. For instance, videotapes of skilled typists show that the way a finger strikes a key is influenced by the keys it is about to strike next. In other words, in skilled activity, actions are not entirely sequential or independent of one another. Similarly, we saw that the actions for page turning were not sequential with reading but overlapped with it so that there was as little disruption to the main task of reading as possible. This sort of strategy appeared to make the mechanics of the interaction faster and more efficient.

We began to see that part of the reason this was possible was that the physical feel of the paper meant that little attention (and especially visual attention) had to be given over to the task of page turning. Much of the information needed to navigate was both implicit and tactile. Similarly, physical cues such as thickness of the document provided important tacit information about where in the document the reader was. All of this being to hand meant that readers were not distracted from the main visual task.

Related to this was the fact that readers relied heavily on the use of two hands to enable the effective interweaving and overlapping of activities. For example, in our videotapes we frequently saw our readers using one hand to keep hold of a page while searching through the document with the other. By marking their place with one hand, they could quickly return to their prior activity. Using two hands also offered opportunities for other types of interactions, such as writing while moving a page closer to read or turning over a page with one hand while using the other to feel how many pages were left. The quick flicking through pages when searching and skimming was also quite clearly a two-handed action, using one hand as a kind of anchor for the actions of the other.

When we looked at the videotapes to see how our readers navigated online, a very different picture emerged. Whether the readers chose to scroll or page through their documents, navigation was slow and distracting—the rendering of the pictures making the problem much worse. This led some of our readers to become extremely irritated:

Online Reader: I was getting very annoyed and clicking on those things and shouting at it. . . . I just found that it took ages and ages. I was losing interest—it was distracting me from the point.

However, aside from these problems of response time, which, after all, have ultimately to do with technical limitations of the computer, another feature that limited quick movement was the fact that any input action made by the user controlling navigation (e.g., clicking and dragging with the mouse) was one-handed. This meant that navigation activities had to be performed serially rather than in parallel with other input activities. The combination of one-handed input with slow system response time meant that interweaving any two activities was cumbersome, as well as making it impossible to perform anything else at the same time.

Spatial constraints on the interface also interfered with quick, flexible movement. For example, in order to move an electronic window, readers needed to first get access to the title bar, which was often obscured by another window. Similar problems were encountered by readers attempting to resize windows or scroll—actions that were also restricted to limited active areas. All these kinds of actions make high demands on visual attention. Any of these little tasks, which are really incidental to the main task at hand (namely, reading), require the reader to look away from the reading task.

So, in summary, we found that navigating through documents is a vital, supporting activity for reading. As such, it needs to help the reading process rather than get in its way. Navigation through paper was quick, automatic, and interwoven with reading. It was as much tactile, two-handed, and multifingered as it was visual.[5] On the computer, navigation was slow, laborious, and detracted from reading. Movement through online documents required breaking away from ongoing activity because it relied heavily on visual, spatially constrained cues and one-handed input.

The Need to Lay Out Information in Space

We saw in the diary study that people often read across documents. That is, they place documents side-by-side and glance quickly back and forth between them. In fact, we found that reading involves multiple documents as much as it centers on a single document. The findings in our laboratory study provided further insight into how people do this and why paper supports it so well.

All the paper readers unclipped the documents we had given them and laid out the individual pages in various arrangements on the desk. Here, we saw how this spatial layout supported the whole range of activities that emerged in the diary study. Multiple pages were used (often alongside separate sheets for note taking) to support the extraction of information from one document to another. They were used more generally to write alongside the document being read. They were used so that information from different documents could be integrated and so that readers could "visualize ideas" (as one person commented). They were also used to check that facts were consistent from one document to another. Being able to see more than one page at a time was crucial to all these activities. But more than this, it was the placing of one page next to another that helped the reader to see structure in a document, to quickly scan through its contents, and to do so in a nonlinear way.

We saw also that readers used two hands to manipulate their paper documents during this kind of multipage reading. Spatial arrangement was dynamic during the reading itself. Readers moved pages in and out of the center of the desk to be brought into the center of the visual field or to hover on the edge of it. Hidden pages would be brought to the front, while others would be covered up or, if needed for quick reference later, moved to a more peripheral region of the work space. All this appeared to take place smoothly and seamlessly in support of the reading and writing tasks.

When we looked at readers who were restricted only to the computer environment, we saw many inventive ways in which they tried to overcome the limited space and inflexibility offered by the interface. As with paper, readers in this situation also talked of the need to lay pages out in order to form a mental picture of the document they were reading. To do this, some of the readers put the document into "Page Layout" mode, which is a way of showing two pages at once. Unfortunately, in this mode, the resolution of the screen was such that the pages were essentially unreadable. At readable resolution, the readers could never see even one whole page at a time. The readers expressed a great deal of concern over this trade-off and talked of feeling lost in that much of the necessary contextual information for developing a sense of text and location lay beyond the window boundaries.

By resizing and overlapping windows, however, some readers were able to see more than one document at a time. But, again, limitations on space and the lack of flexibility in the ways the documents could be laid out caused problems for quick access across documents. For example, there were occasions when readers wanted to use three documents for various parts of the task, but this called for very small window sizes or obscured windows. While "Page View" mode allowed the display of multiple pages, it displayed them in a fixed order.

One consequence of this was that online readers had to give considerable time and effort to selecting and displaying documents in an optimal way. Readers had to anticipate what they would need rather than reacting to the requirements of the task as they arose.

In summary, we learned that, with paper, readers could spread out the documents they were using as they required, changing the arrangement as they undertook their task and using spatial movement to aide their comprehension and navigation. The electronic domain was much more restrictive, imposing limits on where a document could be placed, how it could be placed in relation to another one, and the degree to which readers could visualize and access more than one document at a time.

The Need to Annotate While Reading

A third key finding of this study had to do with the way in which readers marked up documents as they read them. Paper readers extensively annotated the article we gave them to summarize as they read through it. They underlined, used asterisks, and made notes in the margin. The way different readers chose to annotate was quite idiosyncratic, both in the choice of marks and in the ways in which they were used to different effect. For example, some readers used the thickness of a line to indicate the degree of importance of some piece of text, while others used lines in the margin or underlining. Other techniques worked across pages, such as the use of asterisks to link disparate sections of text.

The markings served a variety of purposes. When asked, readers set great store by the ability to refer back to the marks later in their reading and writing activities. They claimed that it helped them to extract structure from the document when they came back and re-read the article, for example, when they referred to the text as they were writing their summary. One feature of such marks was that they relied heavily on the context of the original document:

Paper Reader: The first reading was quite slow and the second reading was skimming. The annotations helped me in the second reading. . . . Whenever I finished writing about some point, I skimmed forward—I looked for the next annotated bit and then I just read around it a little bit if I needed to remind myself of what they were trying to say.

Other readers who marked up the article felt that the very act of making these annotations actually aided their understanding and deepened their comprehension of the text. In fact, although this comes only from readers' impressions in our study, other research supports the notion that note taking helps readers to understand better the text they read.[6]

In contrast, readers who were given only a computer to work with voiced frustration at not being able to annotate the document in some way. Only one of the readers attempted to do this online, using a complex customization of the tool bar to allow him to draw boxes around sections of text or lines down the side of the text. In doing so, this reader experienced a number of difficulties that interfered with the smooth flow of his reading:

Online Reader: So the annotation was not as easy as all that. . . . I think the whole process would have been a lot quicker on paper. Annotations are that much more flexible because you can write in the margins, which you can't very easily do here. You have to establish a new text block and then have to write.

Another reason our readers were generally reluctant to annotate the document online was that this would result in making changes to the original document: bolding, italicizing, or underlining all alter the original document. Readers said that they wanted their annotations to be a separate layer of the document. They were also dissatisfied with the fact that they could not easily make annotations that were perceptually distinct from the underlying text. This distinctiveness they said, was in part what supports quick re-reading by drawing attention to points of interest.

This made it clear that not only does paper support annotation but that these texts on top of texts are important to the process of understanding, navigating, and re-reading documents. However, most electronic document systems do not effectively support annotation as flexibly as paper and pen. It is not enough that one can type in a different color or toggle between texts (although these are useful features in software). Paper-based annotations allow more free-form commentary and a greater breadth of technique.

The Need to Interweave

The last finding has to do with a different kind of writing, this time not *on top of* the text being read, but *in conjunction with* the text being read. We defined note taking in this study as the writing activities that go on either on a separate piece of paper or in a separate electronic document.

On paper, most readers took some notes during the first pass through the document. In general, these notes were made quickly on a separate piece of paper in conjunction with the ongoing reading. Like the annotations, these notes were also used as a resource for referring back to later. However, they differed from the annotated notes in that using a separate piece of paper helped to restructure and pull information together. As one reader put it, it provided "a pool of text and ideas that I can dip into to write real sentences." But the notes were more than this because they were also in the form of plans or outlines that were enriched and modified during the course of reading. A key feature of this kind of note taking was that it needed to be done without disrupting the main reading task:

Paper Reader: The notes aren't in full sentences or anything. They are deliberately shortened so as not to interfere with reading and thinking and things, they are just jottings.

Indeed, a general characteristic of this kind of note taking was its smooth integration with reading. It was both frequent and interwoven

Figure 4.5
One of the participants in the study during the planning stage of her writing.

with reading the science article. This process was helped by the fact that the article to be summarized and the notepaper could be placed side-by-side:

Paper Reader: I always [overlap the science article with my notes] so that you can see and write at the same time; so you are not looking here and then writing over there. You have them together and you just write from one to the other, don't you?

One example of how documents were arranged during this planning stage is shown in figure 4.5. This reader, in the process of writing her summary, needed to refer to multiple documents at once—the science article to be summarized, her notes, and the summary itself. By positioning and overlapping the documents this way, it was possible to make all the information she needed access to, as well as the writing space, available in a compact area.

Placement of surfaces for reading next to surfaces for writing was not the only advantage of paper. Another advantage was allowing independent manipulation of those surfaces. This is important because the optimal angles for reading and writing are quite different from one another. The readers in our study placed the paper at a greater angle away from the perpendicular (approximately 30–45 degrees) while writing than while reading (0–20 degrees). Additionally, we saw that the writing process itself required continual minor adjustments to the paper over time, using the nonpreferred hand as a kind of moving anchor.

Given the unsuitability of most computers for annotating documents, one might think they would be more appropriate for note taking. Online, most readers did try to do this. Two of them took notes using the copy-and-paste function to transfer information from the source text directly into a separate document. They then extensively edited the verbatim text that ultimately became the basis of the final written summary. The other readers typed in most of their online notes only after reading the science article, producing a plan almost entirely from memory with very little reference back to the original document. In all cases, none of the frequent back-and-forth movement between notes and reading was observed as it was for readers using paper.

Restrictions on spatial layout undermined the interweaving of reading and notetaking although online readers did try to approximate what the paper readers did. A commonly used arrangement, especially in the note taking or writing phase, was placing two documents side-by-side with minimal overlap. This avoided problems with the currently active window being sent to the foreground and covering up the other window, which was not only time-consuming but also annoying, such as in the case of this reader trying to alternate between taking notes in one document and navigating in another:

Online Reader: It was annoying that it's got to be the current window in order to be able to move, and the current window is always the one in front. So I can't hide the one I was typing into behind there and simply move the pointer into it and start typing or pasting or whatever.

What these examples point to is the very different styles of writing that computers and paper engender. Electronic cut-and-paste facilities, combined with the relative difficulty of referring to documents while writing in the electronic realm, either put a heavy burden on memory or encourage a different style of writing.[7] On the one hand, with paper it is easier to cross-reference reading material while writing: paper offers flexibility in the reading process. On the other hand, computers make it easier to capture and modify information: they offer flexibility in the writing process. In summary, paper enables readers to interweave their reading and writing activities flexibly and easily. In the electronic world, readers can read or they can write, but they cannot do these things at the same time as easily.

Conclusion

If our studies of reading in the real world had taught us that there were very different purposes when people read and that reading was often part of a range of different activities, our laboratory experiments highlighted the key differences between reading on screen and on paper. Prior to our experiments, researchers had investigated whether the differences between reading in the two media were related to such things as screen resolution; after, we could see it had little to do with the fidelity of text on screens.

In summary, what we learned in the two stages of our research was as follows:

• Reading is part of and embedded within most of the activities that people do at work.

• Paper is the medium of choice for most of these activities, even when the most high-tech technologies are to hand.

• Reading takes on many different guises, is done for a range of reasons, and is done in conjunction with many other activities.

• Reading in real work situations is more often entwined with writing than it takes place without some kind of concurrent writing.

• Reading involves reading across multiple documents as often as it involves reading one document at a time.

• While reading at work is heavily paper-based, it is part of a complex of activities making use of whatever technologies are to hand. This complex varies from person to person and job to job.

• There are characteristic clusters that describe the main kinds of reading and writing people do, depending on the job they do. For example, some people mainly read in order to fill out forms, others read in order to support discussion and social interaction.

These findings challenge the conventional view of reading that says that people read documents one at a time, that people read from the beginning of a document to the end, that they read by themselves, and that they do *not* do other things (such as writing or annotation) at the same time.

When we begin to reformulate what is understood by reading in the real world, we can then begin to understand why paper supports these kind of real-world activities so well. A close look in the laboratory comparing reading from paper versus reading online helped us to illuminate the particular properties of paper relevant in reading. Here, we began to understand more fully the mechanics of reading in a realistic task. We saw how paper played into this task, supporting it in a background way, whereas the computer restricted and distracted from reading and writing. The results of our study have led us to identify four affordances of paper for reading.

First, when we read, we work our way through a text using both our hands and our eyes. We move from one point at the start of the book or report to a later point at the end without always reading the parts in the middle. In this sense, we don't read from beginning to end in sequential order but skip through bits as we see fit. This is especially so with long documents of an organization. (After all, how many of us have ever read one of those in its entirety?) We have explained that this kind of jumping about is a kind of navigation. Though the term is usually used to refer to those occasions when someone is using a map or a compass, we use this term because it describes how when someone reads she will, for example, quickly flick through a document to "get her bearings" before actually starting to read. Having a glance at the conclusion of a management report is, from this view, a technique whereby a reader can decide how much he has to read and how much he can ignore. In these ways, readers do indeed navigate insofar as they determine where they have to go and which way they want to go. And paper is incredibly good at helping us to do this. When a document is on paper, we can see how long it is, we can flick through the pages to see how long it is, we can bend over a corner while searching for a section elsewhere. In other words, paper helps us work our way through documents. It is the tangible properties of paper that support this. Hence, the first affordance of paper is its *tangibility*.

Second, when we read, especially in the workplace, we aren't only reading one thing. We are nearly always looking at another document at the same time. We glance at the document in our hands and then to another on the desk. We sift through a little stack in the out tray to make sure that what we are dealing with now corresponds with what we remember reading last week. We put the most recent document to one side and compare it to another. In a phrase, we cross-reference. This is not to say that when we settle down at our desks we carefully cross-refer between various documents like some detective looking for an oddity or contradiction. Though of course on very rare occasions some people may do these things, reading generally involves an easy flowing and almost unconscious looking at and quickly referring to more than one text. And paper is good at allowing us to do these things. We spread out our documents on the desk, some to the right, some to the left, while we read one in the center. Certainly we can do something similar on the computer with documents in windows that can be placed around a virtual desktop. But somehow—and we all know this to be true—it is more difficult. Documents seem to get obscured. We lose track of where things are. We get a bit muddled. With paper, we don't have these problems. It is the *spatial flexibility* of paper that allows us to do this. This is the second affordance of paper relevant to reading.

Third, when readers are navigating and cross-referencing, they are also adding jottings and notes on the sides of the documents. In other words, they annotate. By this we don't mean the kind of fine examination and associated markings of copy editors and secretaries who are finalizing some publication or an important letter. Rather, we are thinking of how every day, whatever the job or the organization, people use pen and pencil to scribble on the documents they use. Sometimes the markings are underlines, sometimes question marks, and sometimes scribbles that in retrospect may be hard to understand. But doing these things is more than simply a habit. Annotating documents is important because it is part of the process of understanding a document. A third affordance of paper is its *tailorability* in this regard.

A fourth and final reason for using paper is that when people read they are often doing more than simply scribbling at the side of a document. Very often they are also writing a new document at the same time. Paper provides an important advantage here, too. With paper, individuals have no difficulty moving back and forth between the document they are reading and the document they are writing. Indeed, they place the documents side-by-side to support this, sometimes placing them parallel to one another and at other times placing them at odd angles as they think about an idea or make some markings and revisions. Finally, individuals may push one document aside while they focus on the other. It is the *manipulability* of paper that is the key and the fourth affordance supporting this flexible interweaving of reading and writing.

Each of these four affordances contributes to make reading from paper peculiarly effective in an additional way. When people move back and forth through a document to see how long it is or how much further they have to go (i.e., when they navigate); when they glance at another document they have on the desk (i.e., when they cross-refer); when they add little jottings on the side of the paper (i.e., when they annotate); and when they create a new set of notes beside the one they are reading (i.e., when they write while reading), they are *getting to grips with* the information in question. We use this term deliberately. It is as if people need to use their hands and eyes to fully grasp the meaning of the text in question. People really do get to understand what a document conveys by physically getting to grips with it. Given this, the limits of electronic alternatives (at the current time at least) are all too clear.

The Future of Electronic Reading

All this research does not lead us to the conclusion that electronic means are unlikely to have a role in reading activities of the future. Far from it. What it does teach us is that for certain types of reading tasks, *current* electronic technologies do not provide an alternative to paper that is at least as good as paper. Many of these tasks are those most commonly found in work settings. Here there is often a need to cross-refer and annotate; to read and write; and to reflect on and understand the contents of a document. No wonder, then, that readers want—need—to get to grips with it.

But what about reading in other kinds of situations? What about reading for leisure, for example? Our research tells us about what people do when they read at work, but it does not tell us about what they do when they read novels, for instance. Will it be the case that the affordances of paper relevant in the workplace will also be relevant when people read for entertainment?

Figure 4.6
An example of an e-book device designed to support reading for leisure: the
Rocketbook.

This is perhaps all the more interesting because the past few years in particular have seen increased interest in devices and techniques that are
designed to support reading for entertainment (see figure 4.6). The
Rocketbook, and Softbook are just two of the products already on or
about to come onto the market that are intended to replace bound hard-
back and paperback novels. Some of these devices make quite explicit
claims about their paperlike qualities in terms of screen readability, portability, and so on. Most very clearly are attempting to emulate their paper
counterparts in some respects, by maintaining the same proportions of
print on the page, by supporting the display of information one page at a
time (rather than by scrolling), and by preserving visual features such as
margins to reinforce a pagelike look. Some, like the Everybook, even use a
two-screen facing display.

Whether these and similar products will be successful does not depend
upon whether they have paperlike features, however. It will depend upon
whether they fit the task at hand. And here lies the rub. For what we have
seen in this chapter is that prior to our research, there had been very little
investigation into what reading in the workplace involved. Our examina-
tions discovered that it was more complex, more diverse, and more ubiquitous than had been recognized. This in turn led us to identify important
affordances of paper that had simply not been highlighted before.

Now, similarly, very little research has been done into reading for leisure. It has been assumed that the nature of this reading is understood (or, at least, is easy to determine) and that the right design for electronic alternatives to paper can be easily devised. But this may not be the case. Reading for leisure may have unexpected properties and complexities that need to be understood and incorporated into the design of e-books. It may turn out to be the case that doing so will make e-books too costly to be an effective alternative for paper, at least in the short term. It may even be impossible to build them. Consequently, bound paper books may persist even as we progress further into the digital age. Of course, it may be otherwise. But what is certain is that to determine the answers to these questions, more research needs to be undertaken. Only then will it be possible to say whether e-books offer a genuine alternative to paper books and, if they don't, how they might be improved. Ultimately, such research will also help to determine whether new visions of paperless libraries, bookshops, workplaces, and homes are destined to be reality or myth.

5

Paper in Support of Working Together

As we saw in our study of the IMF, one place where paper had firmly found its place was in collaborative situations. Wherever two or more people were gathered together, paper was present. The more intensive the meeting or discussion, the more bits of paper were spread out on desks, coffee tables, floors, and walls. What is it about paper that makes it so suited to the support of collaborative activities? This seemed to us to be a key aspect of understanding paper use. Although the IMF study provided some answers, it was only when we began to look at other, very different kinds of work settings that we felt we began to really understand the issues in depth. Unlike our investigations into reading, it seemed to us this particular line of enquiry could not be investigated in a laboratory. The issues were too bound up with organizational practices to look anywhere other than in real workplaces and at people doing real work.

There are many ways in which paper documents are used for collaboration. They are used to coordinate activities when people work side-by-side or in close physical proximity to one another; they are used in meetings, discussions, and consultations among people; they are used to deliver information to others and to hand over a task from one person to another. And paper documents can be the means by which information—knowledge—is recorded and shared among others. Thus, how paper is archived, stored, and then accessed by others is also important to the process of collaboration.

In this chapter, we cover all these aspects of collaborative work that are bound up with paper. We look at the role of paper

• As a tool for managing and coordinating action among co-workers in a shared environment

- As a medium for information gathering and exchange
- As an artifact in support of discussion
- As a means of archiving information for groups of co-workers

To do this, we describe three studies of very different organizational settings. We look at the work of air traffic controllers, police officers, and office workers in a chocolate-manufacturing organization. In some ways, these settings could not be more different from one another. What they had in common, though, was that all three wanted to move away from their conventional paper-based systems to take advantage of digital technologies for enhanced collaboration. For these organizations, new technologies held out the promise of quick transmission of information from one person to another, the ability to share information more widely, and the ability to better reuse, modify, track, and analyze the information that they produced. However, in all three situations, the problems in introducing new kinds of collaborative systems were much greater than they had anticipated. In one case, the issues were so complex that their attempt to go paperless was abandoned altogether.

The lesson we draw from these different cases is not that paper is always the best medium for collaborative work. Rather, our aim is to show some of the often subtle ways in which collaboration is achieved through paper. This in turn helps us to understand why changing the tools on which collaborative activities depend can radically alter the often deep-rooted processes that revolve around those tools. On a more positive note, it can point to important requirements of new technologies that managers and designers of collaborative tools may not otherwise consider. It can also point to the need for wider organizational changes that may be necessary.

There are two factors at play when we look at the role of paper in collaborative work—one to do with the local, interactional aspects of paper use, and the other to do with broader organizational aspects:

- Locally, paper has physical properties that make it particularly well-suited to supporting some important aspects of collaborative work. These particular interactional properties are not easy to provide with digital media and collaborative tools.

- More broadly, organizational work practices have evolved hand-in-hand with the use of paper. Paper has helped to shape work practices, and work practices have been designed around the use of paper. Consequently, any attempt to move away from paper is likely to entail changes in work practices, too.

Each of the three organizations illustrates differences in the interplay between these two factors. In the first case, air traffic control, we found that paper provides an almost irreplaceable medium in supporting a specific form of collaborative activity in a shared environment. Attempts to redesign the paper-based system failed, and in light of our analysis it seems difficult to specify redesign of the artifacts that would provide as effective an alternative for the kinds of collaborative interactions that go on in that organizational context. However, the example also shows that radical alteration in the broader organizational systems could reduce the need for collaboration, and this in turn would render the affordances of paper much less important.

In the second example, police work, we found that paper affords certain sorts of interactional properties that facilitate the task of eliciting information from the victims of crime. Paper also allowed police officers to control the use of that information until they were sufficiently satisfied with its quality or accuracy. Here we suggest that a more sophisticated understanding of these two roles of paper would lead to the better design of electronic data entry tools. Designers would realize that the affordances of paper that police officers rely on when interviewing are, at the current time, difficult to replicate with electronic alternatives in the form of laptops and other devices. On the other hand, the reasons why police officers use paper as a holding device while the accuracy of information is tested can be reflected and designed into electronic alternatives.

The third example shows that paper-based collaborative filing can be very difficult to replicate with electronic alternatives. Partly this is because much of the paperwork generated in files is not so much an instantiation of knowledge but rather comprises the artifacts that support and reflect the knowledge in people's heads. And partly it is because constellations of activities (not necessarily collaborative) have developed around and with the use of paper files. Here we find that examining closely how the paper files are used leads to conclusions that not all files are alike and that electronic filing systems may be appropriate for some kinds of files and not for others.

The lesson here is not so much about redesigning the electronic tools, or even redesigning the organizational processes, but rather about understanding the work so that new digital systems can be applied in ways that are best suited to the work. It is also about managing the expectations of organizations so that they are more in line with reality when making the transition to digital tools.

Paper in Air Traffic Control

Air traffic control (ATC) is renowned for its technological richness. Technology is important in a number of ways, beginning with the fact that computer-processed radar data constitute the primary information used in ATC. But technology also holds out hope for the future. The hope is that with improved technology, air traffic control can be made safer and reduce the chance of both system and human error. For example, if technology can ensure that the system has the most accurate and up-to-date information about air traffic movements, then it can offer assistance to both pilots and controllers through such things as automated conflict alert alarms. Indeed, it is sometimes suggested that technology may become so sophisticated that in the future ATC may become entirely automated, with controllers having no role whatsoever except to monitor the system in case of failure. However, throughout the world, ATC organizations have been consistently unable to move toward this much-hoped-for goal; all ATC systems have a pivotal role for the human operator somewhere. In addition to this, most often—though not always—along with the presence of human controllers is the ubiquitous presence of paper.

The system operated by the London Air Traffic Control Centre (LATCC) is a case in point. Here, the process of air traffic control revolves around the use of a particular kind of paper artifact called the flight progress strip. These strips are used in many other ATC organizations, though the reasons for this vary. LATCC wanted to reduce reliance on them for a number of reasons, the most important of which was to ensure that the electronic systems had accurate and integrated data about flight movements and flight intentions, which would allow accurate conflict alert systems. With paper flight strips, much of the data needed for such systems did not enter the electronic realm.

But in the case of LATCC, it turned out to be very difficult (though not entirely impossible) to do away with these paper flight strips. The reasons have to do not only with how LATCC's individual controllers use paper strips but with how these paper strips support a kind of teamwork that has evolved over many years. This, in turn, is itself a reflection of the kind of air traffic movement process LATCC operates. As a result, attempts to introduce electronic alternatives to paper flight strips have turned out to be fraught with very profound problems because it is not just the flight progress data tools—the strips themselves—that need to be changed but also the teamwork in those settings and the air traffic movement processes they allow.

The Work of Controlling Aircraft

To explain, we need to look more closely at what air traffic controllers' work is at LATCC.[1] The airspace that LATCC is responsible for (roughly all of England and Wales) is broken up into sectors, each of which is the responsibility of an individual controller and supporting staff. As aircraft move from one sector to another, responsibility for those aircraft moves from one controller and his or her team to the next. Pairs of neighboring sectors are each serviced by a suite of equipment. A suite contains two radar screens (one for each sector), a variety of video display units (VDUs), data entry consoles, printing machines, and flight progress strips, which are placed on racks just above the radar screens in full view of the entire team. Each suite of equipment has its own team. A team typically consists of about five people: a chief, two controllers (one for each sector), and two assistants.

The flight progress strips are pieces of paper about one inch wide and eight inches long that are formatted into boxes containing information about individual flights (figure 5.1). The information is derived from the originally filed flight plans for each aircraft contained in the computer database. In this regard they are historical, but they actually display real-time data because sector suite staff move them about the racks, mark them, and in other ways use them as an ongoing feature of their work. This marking up and physical movement of the strips creates a display that is in effect an accurate representation of what each controller is doing. The entire

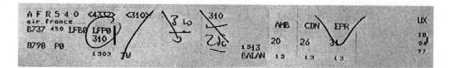

Figure 5.1
A flight progress strip describing Air France flight 540 (courtesy of Wendy Mackay).

display across the racks therefore becomes both the reflection of and the basis for what all those people working on the sector are doing.

To be more precise, the work on and with flight strips is the manifestation of a working division of labor. A controller writes on a strip the particular altitude to which he has directed a plane to descend, or marks the direction in which he has directed it to go. Such markings then enable the chief and the assistants to do their work. They see in what direction a plane has been sent and assess whether that will have implications for an aircraft that is shortly due to arrive on the sector. If so, they notify the neighboring sector controller either by discussing it directly or marking out the relevant strip with a preferred direction or level.

A particular concern of these other team members is to tailor their activities so as to ensure that the controllers do not get overloaded. They look at the strips and at what the controllers are doing, and on that basis assess what jobs they can do. Their concern is not to interfere with the controllers, but to systematically reduce any excessive workload that might occur. If the number of strips that a controller is marking gets too great, for instance, the chief will ask neighboring sector controllers to reduce the number of aircraft they "hand over."

This marking and movement of strips is a continuous process, interwoven with all the activities around the suite. The ultimate effect of this system of teamwork is that a controller is placed in a "cocoon" ensuring that he is protected from high workload and distractions and allowing him to concentrate solely on the job of controlling.

Advantages of Paper Flight Strips
Over the years, numerous attempts have been made to introduce electronic forms of strips in ATC suites. An important motivation behind this is the

aim of maintaining more accurate and up-to-date data about flight movements in the flight progress databases. This would have many advantages, including the ability to automatically link useful applications such as collision alert systems. However, none of these attempts in the past has resulted in major changes in the systems at LATCC. Most were rejected during prototyping and trials. Controllers found that the new systems severely hampered the speed with which they could work and undermined their effective division of labor. Not surprisingly, the staff developed no trust in the new systems.

Looking more closely at ways in which the paper strips are used reveals a number of reasons why they work so well in this kind of collaborative situation. This helps to explain why LATCC found it so difficult to successfully implement new systems.

The paper strips have five important affordances:

1. *Flexibility in spatial layout.*   Paper strips can be flexibly manipulated to indicate a wide range of different situations that might occur. For example, a strip can be "cocked out" (pulled out at an angle to the bay) by a controller or a chief to draw attention to the aircraft in question (figure 5.2). No mark is made on the strip, but its distinct physical orientation vis-à-vis other strips gives it a special identity.

2. *Ease of manipulation.*   The physical ordering of strips may be easily changed, so when variations in actual speeds of aircraft result in their relative positions' being different than planned, the strips can be moved accordingly.

3. *Easy, direct marking.*   Interacting with the paper strips can be easily interwoven with other activities. For example, an advantage with paper is that marking is easy and direct. This means that marking can be done while engaging in other activities, such as discussion with colleagues or with pilots. The ability to do concurrent activities is especially important at times of high workload.

4. *Information at a glance.*   The paper strips can be laid out in a large physical space to provide information at a glance that is simultaneously available to all members of the team. For example, the amount of flight activity in a sector can be seen by the number of strips in a bay: the more there are, the busier it is.

Figure 5.2
"Cocking out" a flight progress strip (courtesy of Wendy Mackay).

5. Rendering actions visible to others.   The use of the paper strips makes
the activities of individuals (such as the process of marking) visible to the
other parties. This is vital because of the interdependence of activity on
and around a control suite. For example, a controller needs to know that
the chief will notice when she marks a new flight level on a strip because the
chief may be in the process of negotiating a hand-over level that would
be affected by this decision. The fact that the paper strips are physically
laid out in space and annotated directly (rather than indirectly through,
for example, a keyboard) means that the activities of co-workers interacting with the strips can be perceived, providing mutual awareness for
collaboration.

Providing these same affordances in electronic alternatives is quite difficult to do. Though some of them can be provided, the key difficulty is providing them all.

First of all, manipulation of the strips—and hence of the information that they embody—is radically altered with most electronic systems. Whereas paper strips can be moved up and down easily, many electronic alternatives only allow this to be done indirectly (through a keyboard or a mouse). More direct manipulation could be provided by a touch-sensitive screen with associated point and drag functions. However, a number of problems would still need to be resolved. To begin with, digital display surfaces only allow two-dimensional representations (i.e., above, below, or beside), whereas paper strips allow three-dimensional relations to be displayed when strips are cocked out. Though one can easily imagine how electronic displays could provide an equivalent (by highlighting the relevant strip in a particular color, for instance), the important point is that paper strips are more flexible. By limiting this flexibility, much of the important information that comes from the spatial orientation of paper strips may become difficult to provide.

If a touch-sensitive screen were offered, it would also need to support direct marking and annotation. The system would need to allow highly variable annotation because controllers' markings can take infinitely different forms (despite there being a "library" of sanctioned markings). The diversity of these markings reflects the range of activities and actions that arise in the natural course of work. Providing both the ability to manipulate and annotate would create substantial processing burdens on an electronic system.

A more fundamental problem is that electronic display media (whether or not they support touch sensitivity) do not provide the capacity to take advantage of spatial layout in the same way as paper strips—information must be laid out within a small, immobile screen. The screens would be small in the relative sense that they cannot be built large enough to provide space for the display of very large numbers of strips. On some busy sectors there can be over fifty strips in a rack at any one time. LCDs might provide a solution here, but they have viewing angle and lighting problems. In any case, for the size that is necessary, their cost might become prohibitive.

A wholly different approach to the design problem could be to break up the provision of flight strips into a set of screens supporting interaction by each of the members of the controlling team. Individually initiated actions could then be displayed on a shared screen. But this could undermine the efficacy of teamwork in the controlling suites. What is crucial about such things as ease of manipulation and ease of marking is that they need to be undertaken in such a way as to ensure that whatever interactions occur with strips, they are visible to all members of a team. It is not only that paper strips provide information at a glance, it is also that any ongoing *interaction* with those strips has at-a-glance or easily visible properties. Paper-based strips constitute the locale for the concentrated and focused interaction of team members; it is the interaction of these team members that supports the cocooning of the controller at the center of the division of labor.

In summary, electronic alternatives may provide some of the affordances of paper strips, but doing so is difficult and costly. Providing them would also need to be undertaken in a gradual and fail-safe way, given that in air traffic control, system enhancements have to be introduced to real-time activities (after early prototyping, of course). And even if the system could be implemented, it would be unlikely to provide a perfect equivalent. The touch-sensitive screen option could be fatally flawed by screen size; the multiple-screen option would break up the concentration of activities that is so important.

The Organizational Context

Given the complexities of moving from paper to electronic flight strips, an alternative approach to redesigning the technological system would be to redesign the organizational processes (something that LATCC has recently embarked upon). We have highlighted some of the important affordances of the paper flight strips in supporting the co-proximate activities of controlling. These in turn allow the cocooning of controllers that we have mentioned. But we also need to recognize that this local work is a reflection of the organizational structures of which it is a part. Creating a cocoon is necessary because the procedures that have been current until very recently for LATCC airspace have made for extremely complex decision making.

There are many reasons for this complexity. As already noted, controllers have full responsibility for aircraft traveling throughout each sector, each of which covers quite a large volume of airspace. Extensive regulations and procedures provide a framework in which controllers operate. However, at LATCC, the airspace procedures do not provide a strict and tidy environment; indeed quite the reverse: at times the procedures can make for difficulty, sending aircraft to the same place at the same time. As a result, sometimes controllers resort to standard procedures to organize air traffic, but more often they must modify these with their own ad hoc organization. Controllers achieve, if you like, order in the sky through the skillful operation of procedures, contingency, and their own ingenuity.

The complexity of such decision making can vary enormously. Sometimes just two aircraft can absorb a controller's concentration; at other times a controller may be able to manage fifteen. What is absolutely crucial at any moment in time is that the controller does not get overwhelmed or, as the controllers themselves put it, "lose the picture." It is the team of individuals who work alongside the controller that ensures that a controller never reaches this threshold.

Paper strips are fundamental to this process. It is the strips, constantly changing and being altered, that are the devices that ensure that the cocooning gets done. Their role in this, their effectiveness as an information representation medium, has developed hand-in-hand with the development of these airspace procedures and work practices. Without paper strips, it would be more difficult to support a flexible working division of labor, resulting in controllers' being less able to deal with complex air traffic control situations.

The important point is that designing out the paper strips is possible but would require reducing the complexity of the work. This might be accomplished by more restrictions in the airspace, whether they be in terms of amount of traffic in any sector or in relation to the configuration of airspace movements that the procedures allow. Indeed, and as we have remarked, LATCC, and more particularly its parent organization, NATS (the national air traffic services of the United Kingdom), have begun to implement such radical changes, and many of these are evident at the new center at Swanick. This is leading to a situation that is very similar to some ATC systems in the United States. Here, aircraft are obliged to fly according to very confined flight paths, in strict sequential order, and on tracks with no intersections and cross-overs. All controllers need to do is supervise the respective speeds of aircraft. For this reason, controllers in these

ATC settings do not need the same support on and around the suites as do controllers at LATCC. In some cases, they work more or less on their own, irrespective of how busy their sectors are. Significantly, they have no need for paper-based flight strips (although, as it happens, they keep simplified copies of them for backup and litigation reasons). This is because the affordances of paper that support the division of labor we have described in LATCC are no longer important. Hence paper is removed from these situations not because technological alternatives have been found but because a different work system is in place.

Paper in Police Work

The ATC example shows how paper can play an important role in the coordination and management of collaborative work in shared spaces such as control rooms. Visibility of actions helps to coordinate the working team. We now turn to a study of police work to see how paper can play a role in supporting the gathering of information through talk. Here, the collaborative work is what might be characterized as discussions between experts and clients. There are many jobs that rely on these kinds of social interactions where a professional is providing a service to a customer by building a relationship with that customer through face-to-face talk. Examples include medical professionals, travel agents, sales people, career counselors, account managers, and so on. In this case, we consider the process of crime reporting, where police need to elicit information from and build relationships with the victims of crime.

Our fieldwork involved studying several police organizations that were trying to transfer paper-based crime-reporting systems to electronic alternatives. In all these forces, police officers ended up adopting a mix of paper and electronic systems rather than abandoning paper altogether. This mix, and in particular the continuing use of paper, was in part a result of resistance to new technologies and to the process of change more generally. But, more important, it reflected the fact that specific affordances of paper relevant to crime-reporting work were not replicated in the electronic alternatives that were offered. These affordances are made salient by looking more closely at the features of the local interactional work involved when police officers gather crime reports.

Police Work and Crime Reporting

Police work involves many things. Police officers have road traffic management tasks and crowd control, for example, as well as custodial responsibilities. But the key task for all police officers, whatever the function or department, is of course crime fighting. Crime fighting involves two aspects: the fighting of crime itself, which involves gathering evidence about crimes, identifying likely culprits, preparing case materials for the courts, and so on. And it involves being the first port of call when someone is a victim of crime. Here the reality is that victims don't just want to know that a bureaucratic process will commence and this will ultimately lead to a conviction; they also want someone to whom they can vent their anger and express their hurt and upset. In short, many want a shoulder to cry on. In this respect, the second aspect of police work involves a kind of social work. These two goals, data gathering and social work, don't always fit side-by-side easily. Indeed, attempts to introduce technology to support one goal do not always help in the satisfactory achievement of the other.

For example, most if not all police forces around the United States and the United Kingdom have introduced new electronic information systems for crime reporting. Such systems enhance the quality and timely gathering of information, allowing its dissemination around police agencies and providing much better search and retrieval capabilities than previous paper-based crime reporting systems. But doing so often compromises and severely affects the provision of the social work responsibilities of police officers. Illustrative of this was one force we studied that attempted to leverage the advantages of electronic crime-reporting systems over paper-based ones by issuing police officers with laptops.[2] These were to be used to enter crime-reporting data when the victims of crime were interviewed. The contents could then be uploaded to a database, either back at headquarters or wirelessly from police vehicles. Quite understandably, it was reasoned that this would make the whole crime-reporting process much more efficient.

Unfortunately, the effect of the laptops was not at all what managers expected. There were two sets of reasons for this. The first and most important had to do with the collaborative process: that is, the interview between police officers and the victims of crime. The second had to do with some design flaws in the overall reporting system.

Turning to the first issue, the collaborative process, here we found that when police officers visit people who have reported crime, or when they deal with individuals at the police station, the actual process of creating a crime report is a delicate matter. It is not simply a question of filling out a form, but, as we have just mentioned, involves dealing with people who are often distressed and sometimes confused. Moreover, it is a process during which the police officer has to give an impression that everything that can be done will be done. For these reasons, the artifacts used to create a crime report are important. In this case, the laptops given to the officers turned out to be entirely unsuitable tools. The officers complained that with the laptops they spent more time working their way through the templates on the screens than they did listening and talking to the victim. "It is awkward," as one of them put it.

When we observed police officers trying to use the laptops, we discovered that their design, shape, input methods, and software did not support the interweaving of the police officer's computer activity with the other activity of continuing the conversation with the crime victims.[3] For one thing, the psychological state of crime victims was often such that police officers had to be extremely alert and sensitive to the ebbs and flows of what those victims said; pauses were sometimes the manifestation of stress as much as a simple mechanical feature of telling the story. These pauses did not necessarily coincide with the movement between various data entry tasks. Nor did victims tell their stories in the order in which police officers needed to enter them; indeed, though police offices tried to steer the narratives, it was often the narratives that determined the ordering of data entry activities.

For these reasons, although the police officers initially tried very hard to complete their data entry tasks online during interviews, eventually most gave up and reverted to taking paper-based notes. As a consequence, the officers were then faced with the extra task of entering the paper information into the system when they had time (either in the patrol car or back at the station).

It is these sorts of matters that need to be fully understood before technology like laptops are introduced into these situations. A police officer who asks for a victim to stop telling his tale while she fiddles with her computer would be undermining one of the very things that the police officer is there for: to allay the victim's fears, to provide encouragement, and to confirm the fact that society will protect him and punish the wrongdoer. Doing so would give the impression that the police officer is more interested in the technology and in getting the data entry task right than in anything else. Needless to say, getting the right information *is* a goal for police officers, and police officers are variously successful at this, but they must not compromise the achievement of the social work task with the data-gathering task.[4] Achieving this balance is one of the unspecified but essential skills of good police work.

The second set of issues that led to resistance had to do with some basic design flaws in the overall system. This reflected a lack of sensitivity to the preceding issues and also to the process of crime data production as a whole. One of the goals behind introducing the laptops was to facilitate prompt reporting. This would enable the force to have the most accurate up-to-date data available and thus be able to more effectively manage its crime-fighting activities. But, in practice, the effect of the system was not as expected. Instead of the data being more accurate, they became less so. The crime reports entered into the system were typically rather rough, omitting important facts and containing inaccuracies. Auditing showed that many reports were continually revised and modified for some time after they were originally entered, and this left an embarrassing impression of a force in which officers were often unable to categorize or comprehensively report crime. This had the politically disastrous consequence of making the force seem incompetent, and this simply added to the interactional problems police officers had to deal with when talking to the victims themselves.

Yet what the electronic reporting system was revealing was not the incompetence of the reporting skills of these officers, but rather the fact that accurate crime reporting is a process that by its very nature needs to unfold over time. The first stage involves meeting with a victim, as we have described, during which some initial data gathering can be done. Depending upon the amount of data gathered or even available at that time, police officers may have to revisit the victim. The reason for this is not only that victims are not always in a fit state to give all the required facts; it is also sometimes the case that the facts aren't available. Some aspects of crime don't always show themselves straightaway: consider how long it takes to determine what has been stolen in a house burglary, for example. When someone reports that her door is smashed down, it sometimes remains unclear whether the incident was breaking and entering or burglary. It is only a burglary when something it taken, and it may take some time for a victim to discover whether something is missing. As another example, cars often go missing and are reported stolen, only to have it discovered later that someone "borrowed" it during a domestic dispute.

In light of this, it should then come as no surprise that what the police officers began to do was to delay entering their reports into the electronic database until they were satisfied with their completeness and accuracy. They did this by reverting back to their original paper forms. The paper forms acted essentially as temporary holding devices to make sure that information was not shared with others or subjected to audit until it was ready. This was not to ensure that it reflected well on the reporting officer so much as to ensure that the crime-reporting system contained accurate data.

Lessons from Police Work

The particular lessons we should take from the fate of electronic systems in police work is not that paper is the ideal answer. Indeed, the fact that, in the force just described, the officers ended up having to create both paper and electronic versions of crime reports (paper during the interviews with victims, electronic versions later on) is indicative of how paper is *not* a medium that provides all that is needed. After all, the electronic versions of the crime reports were made accessible throughout the force, whereas if they had remained on paper such access would have been impossible. The lesson is that no medium necessarily provides the perfect solution.

But even before this can be recognized, work processes need to be properly understood. And this was not done in this case. It is unlikely that police forces are unique in this, and indeed, our research has taught us this is in fact an all-too-common failure in many organizations well removed from police concerns.

If the work processes had been properly understood, the implemented systems would have been better, in our view. For example, crime report databases would have allowed for temporary data to be entered and held until they had been through some form of finalization. Officers could have had a place to enter draft versions, or the ability to mark data as unconfirmed, and so forth. Various types of free-form note taking could also have been allowed for data entry, and this would have helped police officers manage the problem of interacting with victims of crime and computers at the same time. Of course, such data entry methods would still not have been ideal, since some of the problems we have highlighted have to do with flexible and complex navigation, and as we saw previously, current laptop technologies do not provide the interactional affordances to support this.

In other words, another lesson we take from this is that police forces, including the one we have just described, are having to learn that they must make compromises: they cannot implement systems that will allow the production of perfect and timely crime reports without affecting a contradictory goal: to soothe the victims of crime.

Those who design and implement systems for the police need to recognize, then, that there is no neat solution available. They cannot, as in air traffic control, leave paper alone or radically alter the organizational and regulatory structures to make it redundant. They must face up to the fact that though they may be able to introduce some improvements in such things as information sharing, they cannot make the related technologies and processes perfect. But in recognizing that compromise is the best they can do and in being open to which affordances of paper may (or may not) help the balancing of these two goals, they will be in a better position to design what is practical. Fortunately, many police forces in the United Kingdom and the United States have now reached the same conclusion and are implementing systems that offer such hybrid solutions.

Paper in a Chocolate-Manufacturing Company

Finally, we turn to a third important aspect of collaborative work: the sharing and archiving of organizational information. Many organizations strive for better work practices surrounding the storing and sharing of knowledge. As they see it, a major problem is that much of the valuable knowledge that people produce and contribute eventually gets lost, either with the passage of time or because people move on (they change roles or leave the company). Another problem is what is often called leveraging knowledge. This means maximizing the extent to which knowledge is shared among people.

Here, paper is often seen as the medium that shackles the information. In one office we visited, the information technology manager pointed to the filing cabinets and said, "This is the problem—the knowledge is all locked up in these filing cabinets." So the digital world, and systems like electronic document management systems (DMSs),[5] hold out the promise of being able to liberate the paper-bound information from those filing cabinets so that it can be more readily accessed, read, and reused by a community of people. Further, the belief is that such systems will also help preserve organizational information that might otherwise get thrown out or lost.

Yet, as this last case study will show, the problems entailed are more complex than they might appear at first glance. As with police organizations, there is often more than one goal that needs to be satisfied when a document system is put in place. What enables an individual to use a file or set of files may make the same difficult to use for a group; satisfying both may compromise the utility for each. And underscoring these differences are some of the affordances of paper. This is not to say that an electronic DMS cannot provide any benefits—indeed it is obvious it can. But for it to do so requires considerable subtlety when it comes to the process of examining those work practices and related document activities that might be affected through the introduction of such a system.

We illustrate this with research we undertook at the U.K. headquarters of a large multinational chocolate-manufacturing company. The site consisted of the main chocolate factory plus management and administrative functions in an adjoining office building. The focus of the work was to look for opportunities where employees could better share their documents through installation of a new DMS. Four different departments were targeted to be the part of the organization that would pilot the new system.

At the outset of the study, we wanted to understand just what kinds of documents the people in these four departments would want to make available electronically. We also wanted to know what percentage of the existing paper documents that they currently kept at or near their desks we could expect that they would want to scan into the system. This required getting the people involved to sort through all their existing documents. This sorting was necessary as preparation for installation of the system: in order to integrate the new DMS, we had to deal with the legacy documents they already had to hand.

The sorting went as follows. We asked twenty-seven members of staff from the four departments to categorize all the paper documents they had at their desks (including filing cabinets, desk drawers, shelves, and desktops). For any shared paper archives (such as shared filing cabinets) the administrator in charge did the sorting. We gave them five boxes into which to put the materials corresponding to five categories:

1. Scan into the DMS.
2. Keep as paper at your desk.
3. Keep as paper in on-site shared storage.
4. Keep as paper in off-site storage facilities.
5. Discard.

To make the whole process as easy as possible and to motivate the staff, all the materials were then taken away and dealt with appropriately. For example, scanning was outsourced to a scanning bureau.

After the sorting was complete, we measured the quantity of paper in each pile, looked at the kind of documents in each pile, and asked the staff members to give reasons for their categorization. Their responses (table 5.1) surprised us.

Despite the hopes of management for the new system and the motivation of the employees to reduce the paper at their desks, the staff offered up less than 7 percent of the documents to scan into the new system. Many employees were extremely apologetic and even embarrassed about the small pile of materials they had set aside for scanning.

Also worth noting was the difficulty that staff members had in deciding on criteria for scanning or not, and in deciding on keywords to categorize them. Some documents were obvious candidates for this, such as documents that only existed in paper form but that the employees wanted to keep "in case they ever needed them." The same held true for documents that they thought that others might like to access or share.

The fact remained that for most documents people had in their possession, if they didn't discard them, they wanted to keep them in paper form.

Table 5.1
Results of Paper Sorting for Twenty-Seven Staff Members

Category	Average Vol. (cm)	Percent of Total	Examples of Documents	Reasons for Choosing Category
Scan	12.4	6.8	Old project materials, old seminar papers, "tricks and techniques" from outside sources, contracts, nonvital parts of current project files	• Personal backlog kept "just in case" • Documents potentially of value to organization • For reuse electronically
At desk	68.7	37.7	Documents supporting work in progress such as supplier files and current project files, to-do lists and diaries, rough notes and plans, live invoices, personnel files, meeting notes, and meeting preparation	• Offering support for work in progress, e.g., paper offers quick access, markability, flexibility, reliability • Information is personal or private • Difficult to scan items, difficult to print items, or legal reasons
On-site storage	31.3	17.2	Training manuals, course notes, books, business information manuals, computer reference, company magazines, supplier information, maps, phone lists, blank forms, supplier files	• Needs to be easily but not frequently accessible • Of potential value to others in work group • No personal information • Difficult to scan • Most useful in paper form
Off-site storage	12.9	7.0	Old project materials (such as past presentations, data, and notes), details on suppliers associated with past projects, old supplier reviews and surveys, miscellaneous media such as packaging	• Documents kept "just in case" of legal issues • Audit trail of past activities • Document "halfway house" before deciding to discard
Discard	56.9	31.2	Meeting notes, old project materials, brochures from external organizations, flip charts, previous versions of documents	• Unnecessary or difficult to scan items • Was used but is now out-of-date or obsolete • Received but never looked at or used • Copies of same document available elsewhere

Notably, the highest percentage was paper that they wanted to continue to keep at or near their desks, for instance, in shared filing cabinets. As it turns out, the reasons for this shed more light on the affordances of paper. They also have important implications for the utility of electronic document-archiving systems such as DMSs.

Use of a Shared Filing System

To describe the reasons for these findings in more detail, we focus on the largest department we studied, the supplier department. This department was concerned with managing and overseeing the relationship between the company and its suppliers (supplying commodities like cocoa and sugar and also services such as advertising). Members of the department were called buyers. A buyer would be an expert on, and in charge of dealing with, several different suppliers. One of the buyers' key resources was their supplier files—a set of paper files containing each supplier's details as well as past correspondence, meeting notes, records of past and current contracts, and so on.

At the time of the study, these supplier files resided in a shared, centralized paper-filing system in the middle of the department. Managers had targeted this set of filing cabinets as occupying too much space. In addition, they believed these files might be better used if it they could be more easily accessed not only by members of the department but by the company at large. Opinions within the department were quite mixed as to whether it would be appropriate to keep these files online instead of in paper form. Nonetheless, there was a strong motivation to encourage more information sharing. In fact, one of the priorities for this department was to better standardize its processes so that information contained in the filing cabinets could be more easily shared among buyers. Many of the senior managers saw a DMS as a way of facilitating efforts at standardizing its processes and hence encouraging sharing.

A specific example of the kind of document that it was thought might be worth moving out of these filing cabinets into a virtual one was the company information sheet. This allowed the company to gather a full set of detailed information about each supplier. A blank form was sent to any supplier interested in forming a relationship with the company. Once it was filled out and sent back, a new paper folder for that supplier was created. One advantage of using such a form was that it cut down on the clutter and volume of brochures and pamphlets suppliers would otherwise send in. Another advantage was that the form provided a standard format that enabled any buyer within the department to quickly find important details about a supplier.

Like the process of gathering information about suppliers, the purchasing process was routinized. Documents related to this process included invoices, contracts, and the proposals that initiated a business relationship between the chocolate company and its suppliers. These documents were therefore also considered to be good candidates for moving online. By standardizing and making available these documents, it was hoped that any buyer could easily check on the status or find out about purchasing processes (either past or current) regardless of who had executed them or set them in motion.

Thus, there was a well-developed rationale for converting these standard documents into digital form. However, when we began to look through the rest of the contents of each supplier file, it immediately became clear that there were also many *idiosyncratic* documents in each file. These consisted of anything from meeting notes and general correspondence to presentations, brochures, and photographic images of products. Some of these materials were the kinds of advertising paraphernalia that suppliers wanted the company to have to help put their products in the best light (the company information sheet did not allow them to do this). But other materials provided a record of the relationship with the supplier. These included printouts of e-mails, letters, and paper copies of presentations. Many of these had been annotated during the course of meetings and discussions. The annotations included jottings about actions to be followed up, amendments to agreements, further details that came out in conversations, and perhaps most important, comments about problems and issues with supplier's performance not intended for the supplier's eyes.

These materials were idiosyncratic in two ways. They were collected on an ad hoc basis by the buyer who "owned" the relationship, and they were catalogued and filed in diverse (although often systematic) ways reflecting the preferences and knowledge of the buyer. For example, some buyers organized according to type of document, while others stacked their documents chronologically within a file.

Going through these files turned out to be an eye-opening experience not just because it told us more about the documents that buyers collected but also because it began to reveal much more about how they were actually used. Initially, we had been given the impression that the shared central filing cabinet was truly shared in that the files were "owned" and used by anyone in the department. However, it soon became clear that the idiosyncratic organization of each file reflected the fact that each file was in practice "owned" by one buyer, who was not only in charge of the relationship with that supplier but was also in charge of the file.

As it turned out, these files were not often accessed by anyone other than the people who "owned" them. For one thing, anyone other than the owner would not be able to glean much from the file without the owner's being present to tell them about what was in it and how it was put together. This tended to happen only when a buyer was away from the office. If a buyer was going to be away, he or she would brief a colleague on the recent history of doings with suppliers so that queries could be dealt with. The buyers usually did this by physically handing over their currently active files and "walking through them" with the buyer who would be "covering" during the absence.

All of this emphasized that most of what constituted a buyer's expertise resulted from involvement with the buyer's own suppliers through a long history of phone calls and meetings. The correspondence, notes, and other documents such discussions would produce formed a significant part of the documents buyers kept. These materials therefore *supported* rather than *constituted* the expertise of the buyers. In other words, the knowledge existed not so much in the documents as in the heads of the people who owned them—in their memories of what the documents were, in their knowledge of the history of that supplier relationship, and in the recollections that were prompted whenever they went through the files.

Issues for Moving Paper Files Online

The reality of how these files were actually used raised some important issues that did not bode well for moving the central paper filing system to an electronic alternative simply by scanning in the existing paper files. It became clear that even if the files were in electronic form, the fact that only those who owned the files knew how to use them and that the files were more or less unusable without those individuals presented problems for the organization's vision of sharing.

Equally important is that the buyers used the files to support their own activities, not the activities of others. The belief that a DMS would enable these files to be shared more effectively went against the plain fact that these files were *not* a tool or resource for collaboration. In that sense, they seemed to be a poor place to start if the organization was trying to facilitate and encourage sharing.[6] Radical changes in the way the files were used would have to accompany changes in the medium in which they were kept.

Unfortunately, this was not the only problem that we foresaw for the new DMS. We found that even as artifacts to support an individual buyer's working practices, there were other ways the files were used that had developed hand-in-hand with paper:

1. Buyers said that one of the main things they did was to meet with suppliers. For those meetings with suppliers, the paper file was easy to transport and use wherever those meetings took place. Notes could be scribbled during the conversation, and documents could be easily shared and discussed.

2. Prior to a meeting, often buyers would need to remind themselves about where they were in the process, or what had gone on last time they met. As one of them put it, they would need to "get their head round a supplier." Buyers would do this by examining the paper file to see what types of documents were there, the scribbles made on some and not on others, the ordering and arrangement of the documents, whether some were clipped together or bundled into separate groups, and so on. Buyers relied on these various and rich ways of indexing and reminding because they were quick and effective. The structure of the files offered, if you like, at-a-glance indexing properties.

3. These properties showed themselves at another point in the buyers' work practices. They also had to be able to answer queries (mainly by telephone) from clients within the company or from the suppliers themselves. It was a sign of their expertise that if they did not have answers already in their heads, they could quickly lay their hands on the information. Consequently, most buyers would keep the files for which there were currently

active relationships on their desktops, in case there should be calls about them. Just as they rapidly glanced at these files prior to meeting with a supplier, so too would they flick through the same when trying to answer an unexpected query.

4. Physically handing over a file to another buyer was a way not only of delegating responsibility when a buyer was absent but also a visible indication to others in the department about who was going to take on the responsibility. Others would know who could accept queries should phone calls about that supplier arise. They would also know that a file had been properly handed over in the sense that the absent buyer would have talked the other buyer through the contents of the paper file.

These facts made us think long and hard about how to provide support for the kinds of jobs the buyers needed to do as effectively as they could with paper. We concluded that some of the obstacles could probably be overcome. For example, the problem of portability of files could be addressed by making use of laptops for meetings with suppliers. Work flow features could solve some of the problems of showing who had delegated responsibility to another buyer by flagging in the system which files had been handed over electronically to someone else.

But many of the buyers had serious doubts about whether an electronic system would allow them to access information in their files as quickly or as flexibly as on paper—or at least as quickly as they were used to. In fact, their analysis turned out to be correct. When it came to the need for quick access, flexible organization, and rich representational forms for the kinds of ad hoc documents buyers would gather, the DMSs on the market failed miserably. Most DMSs offered only a limited range of ways for organizing documents (such as by date, by person, or by project). Further, documents could not be "clipped" to other documents, placed alongside or next to other documents, or easily arranged in subgroups, apart from using folders within folders. Related to this, those documents scanned into DMSs were reduced to file names, stripping the documents of information that, on paper, could be quickly picked up from the look and feel of the file: the size, shape, color, amount of annotation, thickness, and so on.

These findings, combined with our understanding of how the files were constituted and interpreted, raised serious doubts about the success of moving these supplier files into any of the DMSs that were on the market at that time. At this point, we began to realize that we might have approached the whole issue incorrectly. A new set of concepts were required to enable us to more precisely determine what could be achieved through using electronic forms of the documents in question.

Hot, Warm, and Cold Documents

The example of supplier files in this case study led us to think about the problem of sharing and archiving documents differently, and to think about different kinds of solutions to the problem of moving document collections online. Rather than thinking about a DMS as a *replacement* for a paper-based filing system, we found it more helpful to think about a DMS as a way of archiving only certain kinds of documents.

The rationale for this came from consideration of the way in which the files were used. One metaphor we found helpful here was to think of the files as being hot, warm, or cold.[7] *Hot* files were the files for the currently active supplier relationships: the ones that were currently on the boil, where meetings, negotiations, and discussions were taking place. These were the paper files that sat on the desk next to the telephone, that were handed over and discussed with other buyers because telephone calls would need to be covered. These were usually made readily to hand, or carried from place to place. *Warm* files were the ones not so much for currently active relationships, but for relationships that had been dealt with recently in the past, that needed to be addressed in the near future, or that represented key suppliers in that there were frequent relationship contacts with them over time. Warm files often sat in the desk drawer rather than in the central filing cabinet, or sat in a to-do pile on the corner of the desk. In other words, they often simmered quietly on the periphery of the desk space. Finally, *cold* files were the majority of files: for contracts dealt with long ago, for deals that were done, and even for suppliers that no longer existed. Much of this material was kept "just in case": i.e., in case of legal wranglings, in case a client should ask about past performance of a supplier, or in case that supplier was ever needed again. These files constituted the main part of the central cabinet, although from time to time very cold files would be sent to off-site storage.

It was clear that for the hot files paper was serving multiple purposes. It was for hot files, in particular, that the knowledge about what was in them was very much in the head of the users of those files. It was for these files that portability, being quickly to hand, being easy to organize and search were vitally important. No DMS seemed to provide these affordances. Even if we could have developed a DMS with richer features, buyers claimed they would still print these materials out. We suggested many ways we could build a better DMS: we could provide visual thumbnail sketches of the documents, we could allow more flexible spatial arrangements for organization. We talked of virtual staples, Post-it notes, and annotations. We talked of faster systems that could be displayed on laptops. All of these features seemed promising, but in the meantime paper did its job very well.

For warm files, too, paper played a very important role. By sitting on the edge of the desk, they had a physical presence that served as a reminder of things that needed to be attended to. In desk drawers they could also be quickly to hand. And, when required, they could be treated just like hot files and hence moved about, sorted, and annotated. Some of these things could easily be designed into a DMS: a virtual desktop metaphor could be deployed, for example, to ensure that warm files remained accessible. Various features of the files could be represented in various graphical ways, such as the file owner, who was currently responsible for it, its age, and so on. The trouble was that warm files had either just been hot files, or were about to be, so it was likely that at some point in the near future they would be most useful in paper form, making it hard to justify the time and effort to convert them into electronic form.

The cold files were a different matter, however. These files in a sense had already been put to bed. There were two main problems that filing of cold materials needed to address. First, the owners of these files would eventually move on and hence the knowledge of the processes those documents were part of would no longer be available. At that point, the meaning of the files would be lost. In one respect, this is the crux of the matter for those who have argued that DMSs can help create organizational memory. But what we have seen is that the relation between these documents and the activities they were part of is not self-evident: the documents do not speak for themselves. What this means is that putting a file in cold storage will take work to make its meaning, provenance, and importance clear to others who might want to access it sometime in the future. This work can be made easier in the electronic realm. Tools can be provided to allow users to effectively archive cold documents by adding meaning and context to them. This is not just a case of simple indexing, as we discuss in chapter 6.

This leads on to the second problem. Although the value of a file is, to a large extent, tied to its owner (and an owner who may have moved on), it does not disappear altogether. Certain documents need to be kept "just in case": just in case there is ever a query, just in case there is a lawsuit, and so on. Some of these documents will be legally required to be kept in paper form (although these laws are changing). For these, off-site paper storage seems the best answer. However, when we looked at what was in the cold archives of our buyers, most of these documents could easily have been kept in digital form, saving significant storage space. The digital realm of the DMS seems ideal for these materials, allowing as it does a variety of automatic search and retrieval mechanisms for sifting through large volumes of materials that may not have been looked at in years. A system for linking and tracking related paper materials in off-site storage can also be implemented within a DMS. The off-site storage facility meanwhile does not have to contain anything except those documents that need to be kept on paper for legal reasons.

The conclusions we reached on finishing our work at the chocolate factory was not that DMSs are useless for the situation we studied, but rather, the following:

• The managers of this organization had misunderstood how the key resources of their buyers were used (the paper supplier files), and thus expectations that moving these "tools for collaboration" online would facilitate sharing were wrong on two counts: these were not collaborative tools to start with, and in digital form they were even more unlikely to be shared by others.

• Transforming the paper supplier files into digital form would mean radically transforming the work practices that depended on them. Because the buyers' work practices had evolved around the use of paper, these changes would not only be disruptive, but would undermine critical aspects of the buyers' work.

• The DMS would be most appropriate for archiving cold files, or files that were currently inactive. This would require choosing a DMS that offered good indexing, annotation, and search and retrieval mechanisms. It would also mean instituting new procedures whereby buyers would be expected to put a small amount of work into putting a file into the digital system in the normal course of their work. Similarly, buyers who moved on or changed roles would have to archive any of their cold files in the digital system. This would be as much a requirement of wrapping up the job as talking through with their replacement any files that were currently active.

• For DMSs to be suitable for handling hot and warm files, at least in the kinds of jobs we looked at, they would have to make the transition from paper to digital, and from digital to paper, much quicker and easier than any DMS currently on the marketplace does. They would also have to support much richer and more flexible ways of organizing, collating, sorting, labeling and visualizing those documents than they currently do. Lessons can be learned by looking at the affordances of paper (see chapter 6). These developments will probably not come about for some time.

Conclusion

In the three settings we have described we have touched on many different aspects of how people work together: how they organize their activities and work as a dynamic team; how they make decisions about whether information is ready for sharing; how they talk, sometimes focusing on artifacts and other times wanting artifacts not to get in the way; and how they use documents both for their own individual purposes and for the purpose of sharing knowledge.

In looking closely at these aspects of collaboration, we have seen paper documents in many roles:

• As a flexible medium for the display of real-time information
• As a mechanism for team coordination
• As a holding mechanism for knowledge until it is ready to be shared
• As an artifact in support of delicate, face-to-face interaction
• As support for the retrieval, reminding, organizing, and documenting of an individual's knowledge

• As representations of knowledge that do not necessarily stand alone but that often need additional explanation and context to make them shareable

We have seen there are many different properties of paper that explain why it serves these roles so well. But the aim of this chapter has not been to prove that paper is therefore the best way to support collaborative work. Rather it has been to show that there can be a tightly coupled though often subtle interplay between people's well-established working practices and the paper-based artifacts they use. The reason for this is in part that paper is a versatile medium that can be co-opted, shaped, and adapted to meet the needs of the work. Similarly, work practices have, over time, been shaped and configured around paper tools. The process of change is therefore complex, and one that may be accompanied by misdirected expectations about what will happen and what can be achieved by changing the tools upon which collaborative work practices are based. In the three case studies we looked at, we made very different kinds of recommendations in each case. In none of these cases were the proposed solutions straightforward. In none of these cases did digital solutions confer instant benefits or engender simple transformations.

In the case of air traffic control, the conclusion we reached was that changing the tools would have to be accompanied by major changes in the organizational processes surrounding those tools. In our opinion, computerizing the flight strips would have to involve altering the larger organizational processes first in order to reorient them and integrate them with a new system.[8] In the case of police work, we were able to analyze why initial attempts at introducing computer-based tools failed, partly because alternatives to paper were too intrusive to certain social tasks of police work. Bad design of the system also meant that paper was used as a kind of workaround of the problem of data quality assurance. Better understanding of the data-gathering process would have avoided these design flaws. Nonetheless, we saw that neither paper or digital means could provide a perfect solution for all the intersecting tasks police officers have to undertake, though a recognition of what each medium affords would enable more effective implementations of mixed paper-digital systems. Here was a case for redesign of the artifacts rather than the organizational processes.

And finally, in the case of the chocolate company, we concluded that what was needed was not so much system redesign or process redesign, but applying the technology where it was appropriate. In other words, we found that an understanding of how these office workers were really doing their work allowed us to make judgments about which aspects of the work a new system would improve and which ones it wouldn't.

All three case studies show that the role of paper is much more complex and deeply interwoven with work practice than might appear. The third case study, particularly, emphasized the fact that what people do with paper documents in their hands and in their minds is intimately bound up with the specifics of a division of labor. These specifics and their relation to the affordances of paper are often opaque and difficult to understand even for those deeply familiar with them. That people work in a division of labor can lead people to think that these individuals are also working collaboratively. They may in fact not be doing so. A further subtlety can relate to the fact that members of an office may work individually except at certain junctures, when, for example, they meet and work closely with suppliers.

In light of these examples, it is clear that when an organization attempts to move away from paper, whatever the motivations behind doing so (such as cost, limitations in space, or a desire to enhance collaborative work), it must understand exactly what such a move will entail. Organizations undergoing change need to manage their own expectations as much as the process of change itself. This means being cautious about assuming that sharing, leveraging knowledge, preserving knowledge, and other such desirable outcomes are the natural by-products of embracing new technologies. Only by doing so, can the ideals of new electronic media be realized.

6

Designing New Technologies

Throughout this book we have described a whole range of reasons that people continue to use paper in offices. Most of these we might call good reasons because they make sense given the work that needs to get done, the kinds of goals that people have at work, and the technological alternatives they are faced with. We can contrast this with the so-called bad reasons people stick with paper. These are the reasons that technoenthusiasts like to dwell on: that people are resistant to change, that old habits die hard, and that people and organizations simply lack the knowledge of what new technologies offer. In showing how paper is more than an old-fashioned medium and in drawing attention to the properties that make it ideally suited to certain kinds of activities, we have run the risk of coming out too much in favor of the status quo. We could be accused of defending paper too much, thereby ignoring the great potential of digital technologies. Since we have worked for large information technology companies for many years, this has been a problem from time to time. For example, we have found ourselves at workshops or conferences where our basic message contrasts with those of our own colleagues, who may (quite understandably) be trying to impress upon the audience the ways in which new products or services will radically change the way people work. In this chapter we want to set the record straight. We want to show that our goal is not to lobby for the ways of the past but rather to use our understanding of why people use paper to move forward into the digital future more effectively. In other words, we want to show how looking closely at paper use can be a resource for change rather than an obstacle to it.

Another way of putting this is that over the course of the last few years, we have realized that there is a lot to be gained if one no longer looks at paper as a problem in organizational life. Instead one can treat its use as an indication or a way of learning about how things might be done differently and, in particular, how technology might be better designed. Sometimes this can be a relatively simple exercise. Try looking around your own workplace for paper. Now look at how it is placed next to or on top of, or used instead of the digital technologies. You may well find that paper is flagging a problem in an interface in some device: a fancy new digital telephone has a Post-it note attached to tell us how to transfer a call; an online library search facility has a carefully printed out sign that says "Press F7 to start"; a photocopier has a note attached to the lid to tell us that the error E3 really means a paper jam. Paper, then, can not only draw your attention to a problem but can also provide a quick fix. Sometimes this is all that is needed to help us deal quite well with the technologies in place.

Other times, though, paper can also be used as a fall-back or work-around for problems that are much harder to fix. As we saw in chapter 5 in the case of the police, a poorly designed database caused them to abandon their laptops and revert to pen and paper. The same thing happened in a hospital we studied, where a computer-based system for patient records was so badly designed that doctors reverted to their paper records, only entering data into the digital system later, thereby doubling the amount of administrative work they had to do.[1] And as we saw in the case of air traffic control (chapter 5), the inadequacies of a new system were so fundamental that it was abandoned altogether at the cost of huge amounts of time and money.

These examples are leading us to the central issue of this chapter: the design of new technologies. Our goal is to highlight how looking at paper use in the ways these examples illustrate can point to new design directions for features and functionalities that may be relatively easy to change as well as for longer-term design and development efforts. It can do this because looking at paper use can help deepen understanding of what current technologies can and can't do; where they fall down and where they succeed. This kind of understanding is useful not only for designers and developers of new technology but also for those who have to make choices about introducing off-the-shelf technology into organizations. As we have seen, in many workplaces, new technologies often fail to live up to the expectations of change that people have in mind for them. Consequently, a better understanding of what new technology will and won't do means fewer nasty surprises, better choices about the alternatives, and more realistic expectations about how organizations will use the new systems and devices.

Paper as an Analytic Resource

To get down to practical matters, we use a rather technical term: we like to think of paper as an analytic resource. By this we mean that a focus on paper can be used

• As a lens through which we can come to an understanding of organizational life and the role that document technologies play in it

• As a way of illuminating why alternative tools and technologies may not provide adequate support for the way people currently work or want to work

• As guidance for choosing, designing, or developing new kinds of products, systems, and services that may either replace or supplement paper-based tools

The last point is the most important one. While the first two are about developing an understanding of how people *currently* interact with documents and document-related technologies, the last is about moving forward and making changes.

So, how do we use paper as an analytic resource for design? Anyone who has ever been involved in the design process will tell you it can be a difficult business. There are many choices to be made and trade-offs to consider in designing any new artifact. But design is far from a purely analytic process. It is often just as much a process of inspiration and insight. What we have found is that looking at the way paper is used can help both in the analytic and the inspirational aspects of design. From an analytic perspective, it can help illuminate why existing technologies often offer a poor alternative to paper. This is helpful for the designer, who may then be able to modify the design. From the creative perspective, looking at paper use can suggest new ways forward and new forms of technology that may not exist.

At this point it may be helpful to look again at the notion of affordance. Throughout this book we have given examples of situations where digital alternatives have failed to be successfully incorporated into work practices because they do not provide some of the important *affordances* of paper. By this we mean that paper has certain properties. Those properties in turn *afford* or make possible different kinds of human interaction. Thus, for example, paper is flexible and light, so it affords spreading out on desks and hanging on walls. It is absorbent, so it affords marking on. Further, marks are (more or less) fixed with respect to the medium. This has all kinds of implications. For example, it means that any modifications made to paper (marks on top of marks, attempts to erase marks or blot them out) are visible. On the other hand, these properties also mean paper *lacks* certain affordances. For example, this set of properties means that paper does *not* afford the display of dynamic information. Neither does it afford automatic updating or easy modification of its contents. Put bluntly, when one has put ink to paper, it cannot be changed or rubbed out.

When we think about what guidance this can give us with regard to design, it is important to note that we are not suggesting that digital alternatives need to mimic these properties of paper. This would be to defeat the purpose of making a transition to digital tools. After all, it is precisely because they are *not* paperlike that they open up new possibilities for human interaction. Instead, what we need to do is to consider the next level of abstraction up from affordances. In other words, we need to ask, How are these affordances helping to fulfill people's goals? What is it that paper is doing for people in terms of the work they need to get done?

So, for example, in terms of the preceding affordances, the fact that paper affords spreading out on a desk may support the goal of being able to read across a set of documents and to compare and contrast the information in them. The fact that paper affords marking on may support the goal of making comments and drawing diagrams on a text in a free-form, unconstrained manner. The fact that paper makes modifications visible may support the goal of preserving and showing a history of changes to a document. Note that all these goals could be achieved *through a different set of affordances* in the digital world. Indeed, digital devices could provide new features and services that may make some of these tasks easier (such as automatic data comparison tools). They may also support marking in a paperlike way with the added advantage of being able to search through or rearrange sets of markings. And they can show changes to a document not just through a set of physical markings but also by providing other information about the history of a document, such as who owned it, when changes were made, and so on.

The trick, then, is to consider *both* the affordances of paper and the digital alternatives to ask what together they could provide for the specific kinds of goals people may have. With this knowledge in hand, designers can create *combinations* of the best of both the paper and digital worlds.

We do not want to give the impression that this is an easy task. Depending on the situation, redesign and redevelopment may require a very long time indeed. The difficulty is that sometimes the details of how these goals are supported are often quite important. Added to this, often one needs to provide support for a constellation of goals. Designers need to think carefully about how the features and functionalities they build work together. With regard to this last point, we should also recognize that there may be some situations in which we need to accept that paper *is* the technological ideal for certain kinds of document-related activities because it supports a set of goals and activities more satisfactorily than any digital system could. When this happens, we need to consider the development of technologies that attempt to better integrate paper use with coexisting digital technologies. It is in this way, we believe, that the technologies of the future will offer much more effective support for what people want to do because they will offer the best of what the digital and paper media can provide.

To illustrate these issues more fully, we consider two very different classes of technology roughly corresponding to two broad classes of things that people do with documents in organizations. First, we look at reading technologies. Drawing mainly on the findings from chapter 4, we describe how these can be used to point to new directions for the design of digital reading devices. Such devices are already showing themselves in the marketplace in the form of e-books. We provide a schematic table that shows both the affordances of paper for reading and the affordances of digital alternatives such as e-books. We then go on to show that by being sensitive to the affordances of both, we can begin to create something new and more useful.

The second example considers document management systems (DMSs). These are interesting for a host of reasons, as we saw in chapter 5. Among other things, they are often said to be key to leveraging the knowledge in an organization. The aim of a DMS is to allow people within an organization access to information anytime, anywhere. In contrast, paper documents are stuck in physical space and, once filed, are often difficult to locate or retrieve. As we saw, such a contrast oversimplifies the benefits and problems of each, and not surprisingly, we find that organizations that invest in DMSs rarely significantly reduce the paper they use. Our purpose in this chapter is to show how references to the affordances of paper-based filing systems and archives can help specify how one might design a DMS differently. These affordances can be combined with the affordances of digital systems to create altogether better document management technologies.

Design of Document-Reading Technologies

The first class of technology we turn to is document-reading technologies. Until a few years ago, high-tech designers and developers had not thought of this class of technology as a separate category of device. To read online simply meant reading from a desktop computer or a laptop. Reading in itself was not seen as a special activity that needed to be supported. The last couple of years, however, have seen the emergence of new devices called e-books, which are technologies specifically designed for the reading of books or documents. Typically, an e-book device is a lightweight, wireless tablet with an LCD screen that takes pen or touch input and provides various booklike features, such as electronic page flipping, bookmarking, and highlighting. The kind of reading for which these devices are being developed varies. Sometimes an e-book company will promote its device as one for reading novels. Virtual bookstores provide a variety of new and classic novels to download to the device. In other cases, e-books are marketed mainly as devices in support of work. These devices are sold with software for project managers, students, accountants, and so on. Here the emphasis is on the reading, management, and markup of work-related documents.

To see how an understanding of paper use can contribute to design efforts in the digital world, we now pull together what we've learned about the affordances of paper for reading and compare these to the affordances of current digital alternatives. In other words, we look at what it is about the properties of paper versus digital alternatives that makes possible different aspects of human interaction. Here we consider the desktop PC and the e-book as two interesting cases to look at: one that most of us have had a great deal of experience with, and the other a new alternative designed specially for reading.

The Affordances of Paper for Reading

By studying paper use we have learned a great deal about why people print to read in work situations and the circumstances under which paper serves them very well. As it turns out, this has little to do with the actual clarity of marks on paper versus the clarity or readability of text on a computer screen. The degree to which one technology versus another strains the eyes, is comfortable in terms of glare, and so on is, of course, important. But these aspects have too often been emphasized to the exclusion of other significant issues. Instead, we have learned that what is important about paper in the office environment is that it offers flexible support for many different kinds of reading in ways that digital devices simply have not measured up to yet. As noted in chapter 4, there are four key affordances of paper for reading:

1. *Quick, flexible navigation through and around documents.* Paper affords quick, flexible navigation for a variety of reasons. Because it is tangible, and because marks are fixed with respect to a page, the volume of information in a document is roughly proportional to its size. Readers can literally be hands-on as they move through a text, skimming text, flicking through pages, and feeling where they are all at the same time (figure 6.1).

2. *Reading across more than one document at once.* The fact that information on paper is fixed and yet the medium is light and mobile means that readers can lay out their documents in space in such a way that they can read across an arrangement of documents or pages. They can place them side-by-side, stack them in piles, pull them in and out of the center of the work space, and glance quickly from one to another. This is crucial to many reading activities in the real world.

3. *Marking up a document while reading.* Being able to create a free-flowing, unconstrained set of marks on top of preexisting texts serves important functions for readers. It helps them structure their thoughts while they read, helps them mark out passages for easier re-reading and navigation when coming back to a text, and provides a space in which reminders and ideas can be jotted down in context for later purposes. This becomes

Figure 6.1
Hands-on navigation through paper.

especially important when combined with the ability to spread documents out spatially (figure 6.2).

4. *Interweaving reading and writing.*   Paper supports the seamless interweaving of different but related tasks such as reading and note taking. A reader can place a document for reading next to paper for writing on (e.g., a notebook). Further, the two pieces of paper can be independently manipulated so that each can be placed at the optimal angle for the task at hand (reading or writing). Such hybrid activities are important in many kinds of work situations.

In addition to these affordances of paper, we have learned more generally about the many kinds of reading people do in work situations, how these are very different for different kinds of work settings, and how people use both paper and digital tools to get the work done. In chapter 4 we mapped out ten different kinds of reading activities, ranging from lightweight reading (such as skimming and browsing) to more deeply reflective reading; from reading in linear, sequential style to more goal-directed, search-based reading; from reading in solitary situations to col-

Figure 6.2
Marking up and reading across documents.

laborative reading contexts where reading is often accompanied by talking or listening. We also found what began to look like clusters of professionals who tended to do more of one kind of reading than another.
All these kinds of reading can be carried out on paper, but not all with digital tools. Further, all of the professionals we studied relied on paper in
their activities, but many had difficulties with or avoided the use of digital
tools for certain kinds of activities. This in itself provides a lesson for
design.

The Affordances of Digital Alternatives
Let's now compare these important affordances of paper for reading with
the affordances of current desktop PCs and e-books. In many ways, the
desktop PC has already engendered new forms of reading, such as the
reading of e-mail, the browsing of Web pages, and the reading that occurs
during the online authoring of a document. E-books have naturally developed these possibilities, though their portability offers new features. Further, the fact that their screens are back-lit means that they can be read in
the dark without the need for a flashlight or other ambient light.

One can describe these affordances just as we have with paper. There are five key affordances of digital reading technologies:

1. *Storing and accessing large amounts of information.* One of the big advantages of e-books is the ability to carry around and gain access to entire digital libraries of books and documents. For example, when traveling, one can load up and carry a whole stack of virtual books with no added weight. Keeping the weight and size of the device minimal, then, becomes the main issue for designers and developers.

2. *Displaying multimedia documents.* The PC and the e-book enable not only new ways of reading but more generally new forms of viewing, such as the consumption of multimedia materials including digitized video and audio. To date, of course, most documents, such as fiction books and work reports, do not incorporate such applications. Multimedia documents tend to be confined to such things as encyclopedias. They are also nearly always provided on CD-ROMs. One reason for this is that the volumes of data they require can make them prohibitive to deliver over networks or even on the humble floppy disk. However, the rapid increase in bandwidth and magnetic storage devices, along with increases in the storage capacity of the reading devices themselves, means that the CD-ROM will diminish in importance and be replaced by networked delivery processes. As this happens, many predict that the use of multimedia materials will increase across the board.

3. *Fast full-text searching.* Both PCs and e-books allow readers to search and navigate with keyword facilities. This is done through the keyboard and mouse on the PC, whereas on e-books the requests are entered either with a stylus and handwriting recognition processes or via a virtual keyboard on touch-sensitive screens. Such searches allow readers to find specific pieces of information in large volumes of data very quickly, which is simply not possible in the paper world.

4. *Quick links to related materials.* Both PCs and e-books make possible the reading of text with instant links to other related materials (often called hypertext). This becomes particularly powerful when combined with a Web browser because it enables readers to simply touch or highlight a Web address in order to connect with a Web site. Hypertext also leads to new ways and patterns of navigating through large databases of information.

5. *Dynamically modifying or updating content.* This is perhaps the most obvious affordance of the PC: the fact that digital tools enable one to change the contents of a document and that documents themselves can be updated and changed either automatically or by other people. This means that the digital world can easily make accessible documents (such as newspapers) that do change on a regular basis. It also means that whole classes of activities such as editing and layout are made easier on digital devices. All this depends, of course, not only on the capabilities of the devices displaying the documents in question but also on what kinds of software and input devices are provided (keyboard and mouse are the most common). E-books do not always have keyboards, and none have a mouse, though some do provide virtual keyboards. These are typically presented in a rather clumsy way on a touch-sensitive screen, seriously impeding their ability to support the modification or updating of content.

Lessons for Design

There are many good reasons, then, why people might want to take up PCs or e-books for reading. Yet, as we have seen, for many reading tasks people do not. Let's now examine why this is by looking more closely at how the PC and the e-book fail to provide some of the affordances of paper. More important, let's use an assessment of these shortcomings as a way of specifying how these reading technologies will need to change before people will give up paper. To do this we can say that each affordance of paper for reading can be treated as a design requirement for digital alternatives. These can be combined with the affordances of digital reading technologies to create something better. A summary of the affordances of paper versus digital technologies is shown in table 6.1.

Support for Flexible Navigation   The first design issue has to do with the fact that navigation through a paper document is a direct hands-on experience using an array of tactile as well as visual cues. Navigation rarely gets in the way of the reading task. Navigating on a desktop PC is a different story. The typical PC interface imposes three serious constraints:

• Input is indirect (via mouse or keyboard).

• Input is (largely) one-handed.

• Both input and feedback rely mainly on visual cues.

Table 6.1
The Affordances of Paper and of Digital Technologies for Reading

---

Affordances of Paper
Quick, flexible navigation through and around documents
Reading across more than one document at once
Marking up a document while reading
Interweaving reading and writing

Affordances of Digital Technologies
Storing and accessing large amounts of information
Displaying multimedia documents
Fast full-text searching
Quick links to related materials
Dynamically modifying or updating content

Consider the use of the mouse for scrolling. The user has to visually locate the scrollbar, position the cursor over a relatively small area, and then perform a series of mouse clicks alternating with glances at the displayed page to navigate through the document. Using the mouse for navigating also means that any other kind of input (such as text editing) cannot happen at the same time. Because input is serial and visual, it cannot help but detract from whatever the main task of the reader is (be it browsing, skimming, or checking the contents of one document against another). Even knowing where you are in a document requires looking at visual cues such as page numbers or the location box in the scrollbar.

There are other factors that undermine readers' sense of knowing where they are in a PC document. The limited screen size of the PC means that readers generally only view one page at a time and usually do not see a whole page. Anything outside the window is truly occluded from view. E-books have smaller screens, so one would think this would be even more of a problem. But e-book designers have tried to get around this problem by reducing the font size of printed text as well as the page size to suit the e-book screen. In other words, they have just made pages smaller. Contrast this with a paper book, where even though we are focusing on what we are reading, what has gone before and what is yet to come is in our peripheral vision. The book itself and the pages on which it is inscribed become the context for whatever bit of text we are engaged in reading. Not so in the case of a PC or e-book window. As Geoffrey Nunberg put it, "Reading Proust in a window is like viewing Normandy through a bombsight."[2] PCs and e-books force us into a kind of tunnel vision situation.

Coupled with this, we know that readers of paper documents do develop a kind of spatial memory for where things are in a physical book, and our own work has shown that the dynamic scrolling of text inside a window interferes with the ability to construct this mental picture. However, we did find that people would develop a similar kind of spatial memory if paper pages were simulated online—in other words, if a document were presented on a screen with "fixed" electronic pages and simulated page flipping for navigation.[3]

E-books do improve the situation over PCs. For one thing, most have adopted the model of electronic page flipping, which helps confer some of the benefits we have mentioned. Most also improve on input techniques for navigation. They have buttons, usually by default on the left side of the screen, which perform fast page flipping through a document. This means that a right-handed person can flip pages with the left hand while holding the pen in the right hand to mark up the text or perform other kinds of input tasks. It is not strictly two-handed parallel input but nonetheless allows the hands to be in two convenient places at the same time. Also, the use of physical buttons means there is less demand on the visual system, which can then be given over to other tasks.

Nonetheless, for most e-books, the cues about where one is in a virtual document are still primarily visual. These visual cues are also provided within the limits of a small screen. With most e-books, the reader sees only a single page and must infer from that how far into a document that page is by relying on visual indicators such as scrollbars, page numbers, and so on. Knowing where you are is not a matter of directly sensing one's place through various tactile cues. Similarly, the extent to which such e-book interfaces truly support various forms of two-handed input is quite limited.

What the affordances of paper teach us about the design of digital devices, then, is that navigational techniques need to be developed that place fewer demands on the visual system so that they interfere less with the main tasks of reading and writing. This can be accomplished in several ways: providing richer nonvisual cues, providing more direct forms of input, and supporting more extensive two-handed input.

First, consider that interfaces can make much more use of the other perceptual channels, such as providing more audio cues to users. Subtle, natural sounds such as the sounds of paper being flicked through can be synthesized and used to reinforce users' actions, including flicking through pages. Natural sounds can also be used to indicate, for example, the thickness of a document: here the sounds of different thicknesses of wood are very effective at conveying the thickness of a book (something you must try to believe!). Such feedback could be provided in the natural course of navigation so that the cues are picked up while the user does other things. This kind of audio cue has been used with great effectiveness in an early research prototype for the Apple Macintosh.[4]

Second, in order to lessen demands on the visual system, more tactile controls would be of great benefit. For example, physical sliders, buttons or pressure-sensitive textured areas of the frame could be used for controlling various navigational activities such as riffling through pages, place holding, or toggling between different documents. This would allow users to feel more directly where they are rather than forcing them to look.

Third, the interface could provide support for much richer two-handed input. Not only should e-book interfaces allow such input and control but they should encourage it. Two-handed input could support a whole range of new navigation techniques, such as using one hand to mark one's place in a document while scrolling or page turning with the other. This would also allow for the support of concurrent activities like writing on one document while navigating in another.

A fourth and final aspect to consider is the actual visual layout of the information. Designers need to think carefully about how they could provide more visual context for giving readers a sense of where they are in a text. One obvious solution is that a bigger screen or even two screens could display two pages at once. But there may be ways of providing more context by using clever visual cues even within a single screen. For example, three-dimensional graphics could represent the thickness of a document around the edges of a page. Pages gone before might be represented as a thumbnail or by some graphic along the left side of the screen.

Support for Cross-Document Use   A second important issue for design comes from looking at the way in which paper supports the use of multiple documents, in particular the reading across documents so common in the workplace. Desktop PCs on their own do a very poor job of supporting these kinds of activities. Consider how a PC allows users to lay out documents. Whereas paper is a mobile medium displaying fixed information, a desktop PC is an immobile medium displaying dynamic information. Any document layout, then, must take place within a rigid physical frame. Because of the limited screen size, there are significant constraints on how many pages or documents one can make visually available at once. This fact, combined with limited ways in which one can lay out two or more documents within that display, makes it very difficult to quickly interact or read across more than one document or page at a time. Overlapping windows often obscure each other; side-by-side configurations can be hard to see properly because they need to be quite small to display two pages at once; and so forth.

E-books, too, are generally speaking poor at supporting the display of multiple documents. With the exception of one or two products that have two display screens, e-books are not only limited to a single screen but use screens that are significantly smaller than a desktop machine. It is as if the designers of e-books have given no consideration at all to how a reader would look at two pages at once, two documents at once, or even quickly move between two documents. Without the ability to view at least two documents or pages at once, no e-book could be taken seriously as a reading device for work.

What this points to is that even though e-book developers might be loathe to add to the cost and weight of their devices by providing two screens, there are important if not crucial benefits to be gained by doing so, at least in terms of a reading device for workplace use. With two screens it becomes possible to display two documents at once. Even better, the two screens could communicate with each other, and allow operations across documents, such as cutting and pasting, comparison, and search facilities.

If e-books were redesigned in this way, users could easily accomplish many tasks on-screen without the need of paper. Consider the following activities:

• Reading a document on one screen and writing a to-do list or a plan of action on the other

• Copying bits of information from a document on one screen and filling out a form on the other

• Looking for general ideas and themes in an old report to help in composing a new one, and copying across formats, acronyms, and expressions

• Pointing to one version of a document to highlight any differences in another version

• Reading a draft someone else has reviewed and incorporating those changes into one's own master copy

• Composing a letter on one screen by referring to a letter received on the other. Automatically cutting and pasting details such as the sender's address or any facts and figures he refers to

Of course, designing these affordances into an e-book will increase cost, and this may be a major obstacle given that it is only recently that e-books have come down to affordable levels. There may be ways of supporting some of these same kinds of goals without drastically increasing cost, however. Some of these requirements can be supported with a single screen:

• Quick toggling between two or more documents.

• Thumbnails of other documents available at the periphery that can be easily clicked on to zoom in and out of focus.

• Experimenting with different ways of displaying large collections of documents within a limited space, such as fisheye views, transparent layers, and three-dimensional display.

• More flexible ways of placing and displaying multiple documents within a screen. This ranges from simple suggestions like removing constraints on readers' ability to lay any two pages side-by-side to the possibility of placing documents and pages in virtual piles or even at angles to each other. Key to this would be allowing users to use two hands to control the documents in question, much as we do on our real desktops.

Support for Annotation While Reading   A third requirement for a digital reading device is the ability to mark-up documents while reading. This may be for annotating documents while reading them, taking notes in the course of reading, or even form filling while reading.

Here the desktop PC is fundamentally different from paper in that marking primarily takes place via the keyboard. This means that comments or annotations on top of preexisting texts tend to alter the spatial layout of the text underneath. This is wonderful for doing actual editing, but it simply does not work for the whole range of activities we have out-lined that people do when they read. Admittedly, various software pack-ages have tried to address this by adding features whereby a user can turn on the "revisions feature," which shows comments in different colors. Vi-sual representations of the nature of the changes can also be provided. Such tools can be extremely useful when co-authoring a paper, for exam-ple. However, there are other times when making actual changes is not the goal. Rather the goal is to draw attention to aspects of a text without mak-ing changes.

The key issue is that there are constraints inherent in keyboard input. Though keyboard entry makes PCs ideal for authoring, it is not so good for marking while reading. Many of the marks readers prefer to make do not involve text but rather making pictures, arrows, and lines. Further, such marks can be made anywhere and are not restricted to areas where an elec-tronic page will accept input. This means that a user can choose to put those marks where she thinks they will be most effectively noticed, whether it be at the top of the page or even sometimes right through an of-fending paragraph. The point is that pen and paper support flexibility in this area, whereas the PC with keyboard entry does not.

Most e-books have successfully attended to this affordance of paper. Most recognize not only the importance of marking while reading but pro-vide pen-based input, too. The portability of the e-book and the fact that it can be used flat on a desktop also make it well suited to stylus entry. Pen-based input naturally allows users to make free text annotations as well as make marks in context and as a distinct layer on top of typed text. Many features that e-books provide also emulate what is done in the paper world, such as the ability to highlight text, make notes in the margin, cre-ate Post-it notes, and so on. Further, digital marking techniques offer many interesting advantages over paper by allowing readers to choose whether the annotations are to be permanent or temporary, by offering se-lective viewing capabilities according to who wrote the marks and when, or by actually allowing marks such as proofreader symbols to effect changes in the underlying text if desired. Many such features can be found in research prototypes such as FXPAL'S XLibris notebook (figure 6.3) and a prototype collaborative writing system developed at Xerox PARC called MATE.[5]

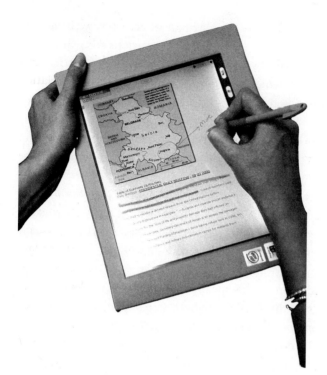

Figure 6.3
FXPAL's "XLibris" reader's notebook, showing annotation of a document while reading.

It is still the case, though, that marking on a tablet is a different and generally speaking inferior experience to marking on paper. Part of the problem lies in screen resolution and size. This means that writing needs to be made bigger than on paper to make it readable. In any case, small screen size means there simply isn't space to write as much as a reader might want to. Mostly she is restricted to margins. Beyond this, there is also a perception that writing on a screen doesn't "feel as good" as writing with pen and paper. These are not merely subjective feelings. Screens typically make the user feel he is not truly making contact with the underlying text. The user is right. Most screens suffer from various degrees of parallax: where the user sees the pen touching the screen is not where the mark is actually displayed. This is a function of the layers of an LCD touch-sensitive screen.

What the user touches is not the same as the part of the screen that displays marks.

Technical enhancements will very likely improve all these aspects of pen-based interaction with e-books. And here, it is clear to us, emulation of paper is the right way forward. There are some good stylus-based systems already, although not in the context of e-books. Some have pressure-sensitive pens that do feel much more like a pen on paper because as one presses more firmly, the line becomes thicker. Unfortunately, at the current time consumers are typically faced with a choice between devices that support keyboard entry (the laptop) and those that support pen-based entry; there are only a few that give the user a choice. Because readers often want to take notes as well as annotate when they read, a detachable keyboard accessory for an e-book would be quite valuable. Also, pen input for laptops might add value in the realm of reading tasks.

Support for Interweaving Reading and Writing   A fourth requirement we have already touched on: namely, the need to support the easy interweaving of various kinds of reading and writing. The PC is not well designed for this. For one thing, it does not accept parallel input. So if a reader wants to, say, flick through one document while taking notes in another, all of the activities have to be performed serially. Any of these input actions may cause distracting things to occur, such as bringing one document window forward to obscure another, invoking a long response time for the system to perform the action, or requiring the user to change modes to perform certain kinds of input activities. Many actions are also constrained to small active areas on the screen, which means more of the user's attention is taken away from the main task.

E-books are generally better in that they allow users to add comments on preexisting documents. But this is only one of the multiple activities people do when reading. For example, e-books do not allow the kind of writing that often goes with reading (such as note taking) where the writing requires a separate space. E-books do not support the full range of reading and writing tasks that one finds in reading-based activities, especially in the workplace. Here our previous comments about the potential value of two screens again become important. Many of the examples we gave involved the use of one display primarily for reading and the other display primarily for writing. In a pen-based interface, as is provided with most e-books, this suggests another interesting possibility. We know from our own work that readers will place a display at different angles when writing than when reading.[6] This suggests that to optimize the two-display design, a two-screen e-book should ideally provide detachable screens so that they can be separately manipulated. The screens would then need to communicate with each other either via a flexible tether or (a less constrained solution) in a wireless way. Users could then position each screen any way they wanted to, and juxtapose the two screens in the most effective way for whatever task is at hand. This might mean placing them side-by-side, at angles to each other, or placing one upright for reading while the other lies flat on the desk or lap for writing.

Specialized Devices: Support for Different Kinds of Reading   Whereas paper has four affordances that support reading, there is a fifth way in which the design of electronic alternatives can be improved. This has to do with the fact that there are many kinds of reading. PCs, for example, can provide more than adequate support for some kinds of reading, especially reading short self-contained pieces of text or reading to edit. As we have seen, though, problems can occur when doing other kinds of reading, such as deep reflective reading (especially of long texts); reading for the purpose of writing; reading to integrate information from multiple documents, and reading to critically review a document. The PC fails to provide the necessary affordances for these tasks. This is why people resort to paper when they do these things.

There is therefore a general message for designers of digital reading devices: it is vital to understand precisely what is meant by "reading." When we looked in depth at the reading habits of fifteen very different professionals, we saw that even in that small sample, we could cluster these individuals according to the main kinds of reading and writing that they tended to do. So, instead of designing generic reading devices, it might be that designers need to develop a range of different reading devices aimed at different kinds of professional audiences.

One of the clusters we identified comprised primarily form fillers, whose main reading task was one of searching through documents for facts, results, instructions, and other specific kinds of information in order to complete forms. As it happened, most of the people in this group were medical professionals, but there are doubtless people in other domains who would fit this profile. For the people we studied, we found that this kind of document activity was typically something they did on their own, although the documents they interacted with were generally jointly authored.

This suggests the need for a kind of reading device specifically geared toward providing users with an armory of different kinds of flexible search and navigation features. This would be ideal for people whose main reading task is either quickly browsing through information or finding and getting access to specific kinds of information. Digital devices have the potential of conferring many benefits over and above paper here, especially in terms of offering greater access and more up-to-date information. This would be particularly valuable in settings such as hospitals, where paper documents like patients' notes are often out-of-date and where information needs to come from many different departments.

A second interesting group of subjects was made up of people who spent a great deal of time reading before, during, and after meetings and discussions. This includes prereading activities, referring to and marking up documents during face-to-face talking, and reading prepared slides during presentations. The cluster we looked at contained a senior lawyer, a marketing manager, a startup executive, an optician, and a social worker. In other words, these workers could be characterized mainly as middle or upper managers or as people who work mainly with clients. Such people spend a great deal of time viewing or reading documents with others. Having said that, they also engage in very different kinds of writing activities. For example, the optician mainly spent time form filling as a result of discussions with clients, whereas the social worker mainly took freehand notes. The marketing manager relied very heavily on the annotation of the documents around which discussions revolved in order to record pertinent facts or write reminders for herself.

This suggests that another kind of digital reading device is one that is designed with collaborative use in mind, and in particular the joint viewing of documents. This will affect both hardware and software requirements. For example, careful consideration needs to be given to how documents can be looked at together in face-to-face meetings. For an e-book type of solution, the viewing angle and size of the screen will be issues here, as well as the ability to prop up a screen or easily hook it up to a projector. For joint marking of a document, there is a need to explore the range of possibilities that allow multiple pen input and to provide software that supports collaborative marking and editing. People in meeting situations are also frequent document "exchangers," so methods of easily allowing people to electronically hand over documents to others—for example, by wirelessly "beaming" them from one device to another—would also be a valuable feature.

The third cluster we observed is what we might call cross-referencers. These are people who spent most of their reading time working across multiple documents. Examples include accounting assistants, who spent most of their time cross-referencing to check for consistency among figures; pilots, who mostly spent time integrating and extracting from multiple documents to plan routes and check flight information; and lawyers, who mostly cross-referenced to check language and format of documents in the creation of new ones.

This group of cross-referencers suggests that some people may be more heavily in need of multiple display surfaces than others in their work. Thus, a two-screen version of a device might well find its niche naturally within some professions. However, judging by the degree to which multiple displays were used across our whole sample, we can surmise that at least two functionally interlinked screens might be more generally useful, for the whole range of reasons we have outlined.

The Future of Paper for Reading

In chapter 1 we noted that one place where the idea of the paperless office was propagated was Xerox PARC. It was here that the first networked, window-based system was devised. Since that time PARC has, of course, moved on to research newer technologies. Some of these technologies are for reading. These technologies are still only concepts and illustrations rather than products, but they are interesting in a number of ways. Above all, they have been developed so as to make people think about how fundamental assumptions underscoring current reading practices may be altered and transformed.

For example, the Tilting Table allows a reader to manipulate a document presented on a moving table top in such a way that he can move rapidly between and across documents simply by tilting the table one way or another. This technology, combining an overhead projector and a table or screen mounted on pneumatic shocks that track movement, is intended for very large documents—wall-sized plans or images or even text the size of billboards. Its purpose is to provoke ideas about what it means to navigate through large amounts of information and what may be the physical relationship between a reader and the documented forms of the information. Another concept, called the Walk-in Comix, provides something similar. Wall-sized screens of cartoons surround a reader, and these are linked to create a series of rooms. A reader must navigate his way through the rooms to work their way through a story.

Both the Walk-in Comix and the Tilting Table illustrate how reading with hands and eyes might be transformed. With the Walk-in Comix, the reader has to use his legs as way of navigating; with the Tilting Table the reader must alter his relationship to the angle of the reading surface to move through the text, and such movements may not be linear and sequential but sideways, backwards, forwards, even downwards.

While lauding such research—and indeed research carried out on the future of reading in other research centers in Silicon Valley and elsewhere—it is, in our view, one step beyond what we need to concern ourselves with now. We believe that before such technologies can transform reading, one needs to make sure that the technologies we see on the marketplace in the next few years are much more usable than the current crop of PCs and e-books.

In particular, reading technologies need to incorporate the most important affordances for reading that paper currently provides. Accordingly, digital reading devices need to offer much more than simply a portable screen. They need to offer tactile controls that support navigation, such as buttons and physical sliders. They need to use natural sounds to aide navigation, such as the sound of flicking through pages. In addition to this, we have seen that reading in the workplace typically involves more than one document and often involves annotation while reading. Therefore, digital reading devices need to consist of more than one screen or incorporate multiple-screen techniques for moving between documents. Similarly, reading devices need to allow people to write more effectively as they read—as we saw, people often compose notes and briefs while reading.

These requirements have led us to argue that the most effective way of providing what readers need in the workplace is to offer them different types of reading devices depending upon the types of work they undertake. Key to this view is that it is the types of interaction people have with the text they read that distinguishes one type of reader from another and that should distinguish one type of reading device from another. Thinking of the future of e-books and digital reading devices in this way, though, does not mandate a reading appliance for every type of professional or occupational group. One of the difficulties of that strategy is that the resulting technologies can be focused too much on one domain or work group and so not be generic enough to ensure that sufficient resources are allocated for development and marketing. A likely result is that these technologies would end up not being good at their intended domain nor usable more generally. Our view suggests that the future of reading will consist of a few generic devices rather than many appliances. The three we have described might correspond to these classes: the form-filling device, the collaborative reading device, and the cross-referencing device.

Even so, this means that much more research and technology development will need to be done. Current e-books are way off the mark when it comes to offering the kinds of tools that people need in the workplace. Once this is done, however (and we are convinced that it can be), the future will be one in which the technologies we see in the office will be much more flexible than they currently are. One will see screens lying aside one another, perhaps at different angles, as readers cross-reference; one will find people picking up their screens and using two hands to work their way through documents, sometimes touching the screen and sometimes using buttons on the side of the device to move through the documents in question. In this way they will be, quite literally, *getting to grips* with information the way they currently do with paper.

But it has to be said that we don't think that these kinds of improvements will lead to the disappearance of paper. We think paper will still be used extensively for the final form of various types of documents. At that point, the kinds of affordances electronic tools offer, the ability to annotate and modify, to link to other documents and allow the creation of new documents, may be less important than having a unified and bounded object.[7] After all, once a document has been finished, the physical boundaries of paper often come to define its intellectual and organizational boundaries, too.

By the same token, we don't think that novels and leisure reading will move into the electronic world anytime soon. Despite their efforts to emulate some of the tactile properties of paperbacks, e-book manufacturers might be missing the point: paper may already provide an ideal medium for leisure reading. This is not to say that e-books will never enter the home or be placed on the bedside table. We are sure they will be, but not as surrogate paperbacks. Rather, like the technologies that Xerox has been researching, the new forms of e-books and other reading devices will afford new forms of reading and new kinds of leisure activities. Already one finds hand-held, Web-browsing devices: these are offering a new kind of a leisure activity that can be carried out on the couch. It is our view that e-books will not replace traditional paperbacks in terms of function but rather offer different functions for different kinds of activities.

Design of Digital Document Management Systems

We now move on to quite a different class of technologies to see what we might learn from the world of paper for the purpose of design. This class of technology is often called a document management system, but here we are talking more generally about software (and often accompanying bits of hardware) that allows people to store, search, access, manage, and share documents in the digital realm, whether the documents originated on paper (in which case they need to be scanned in) or whether they were created online. The networked desktop computer, of course, enables all these document activities to some extent, but the difference with DMS software is the emphasis on document sharing within an organization. A DMS promises to benefit an organization by transforming documents from paper objects owned by individual people into a collective electronic resource that can be accessed and used by all.

In keeping with the emphasis on sharing, DMSs provide tools to input, process, search, and store large collections of documents. Such systems vary in the extent to which they are seen as archiving versus management systems. Archiving systems put more emphasis on how one inputs and preserves the documents (including scanning), how one indexes or categorizes them (sometimes automatically), and how one searches large volumes of information. Management systems are more likely to have digital work flow capabilities, which means that they provide facilities to automatically route documents from one person to another and allow users to review, add comments to, and mark the status of documents before passing them on to someone else. More and more DMSs are now Web-based, but many are also server-based. There are generic DMSs on the market (e.g., Lotus Notes, Xerox's Documentum), but often large organizations commission custom-made solutions to suit their own particular needs.

We describe here what our studies have found to be the key affordances of paper for the management, sharing, and storing of documents, and compare these to the affordances of most digital DMSs. Of course, DMSs vary widely in the kinds of functionalities and features they offer. As a result, some of our criticisms of DMSs may be unfair to particular systems, and some of the praise undeserved. But there are some generalizations we *can* make about the paper versus the digital world for supporting these kinds of document activities. What we find is that most of the affordances of paper are ideally suited for supporting what people do with hot or warm files (see chapter 5). Hot files are those that people are currently working with, those that support activities in progress. Warm files are those that have just recently been used or which are about to be used. These hot and warm documents can be contrasted with the majority of files that exist in most workplaces—the cold files. These are the files and documents for activities in the past. Often these archived documents are kept "just in case" they are ever needed. As it happens, the affordances of digital systems such as DMSs are much better suited (or could be made much better suited) to the support of activities with cold files.

The Affordances of a Paper Filing System
We've learned a number of valuable lessons about how people manage, store, and share documents in the paper world. One of the first myths we encountered was one that we heard on visits to many different kinds of workplaces: namely, the belief that people don't share information be-

cause it is "locked up" in the paper world. If only this information were in electronic form, this myth goes, it would be more widely accessed and shared. What we found was that when one actually examines the paper that organizations receive through the mail or the paper that people keep at their desks, the owners of that paper usually decide that a large part of it is not worth the effort of scanning into a digital system. Our first inkling of this was at DanTech (chapter 2), where plans to scan all incoming paper mail into their electronic filing system were soon abandoned. This was later backed up in our study of the chocolate-manufacturing company (chapter 5), where we found that when we asked people to sort through the paper files at their desks, they set only 7 percent of it aside for scanning into a DMS. Most of the paper they either wanted to throw out (31 percent) or keep as paper at their desks (38 percent).

There are two very interesting reasons for this. First, much of the paper that gets sent to organizations, and a lot of the paper that people keep, is deemed to be junk—either it is judged not valuable from the outset or it becomes obsolete with time. Scanning it in would therefore be a waste of time and energy.

Second, and more important, many documents are judged to be more useful in their existing paper form than they would be in electronic form. Delving into this second point helps illuminate several different affordances of paper in relation to the use of office files. These are bound up with the nature of information that people keep and use in supporting their day-to-day work.

Controlling Access Until Information Is "Ready"   One of the most important findings is that paper often serves as a useful holding place for information until it is ready to be shared electronically with the rest of an organization. This arises in several different situations, for slightly different reasons.

In the case of account managers at UKCom (chapter 2), for example, we saw that information might be sensitive and private, being the product of notes taken during a series of dinners with clients. These notes were valuable to the account managers in their role as relationship builders, but they were thought to be difficult to understand by anyone without the background knowledge of that relationship. Comments might be taken the wrong way or be seen as potentially libelous, so account managers were reluctant to make these notes available electronically. In the case of the police (chapter 5), we saw another way in which paper was used to hold back information until it was ready for sharing. Here we found that crime reports often took several days or weeks to reach a state where they were complete and accurate. This occurred for a host of reasons, not least because details about events often unfolded over time. As a result, crime reports were largely held on paper until they were ready to be entered into the electronic system. And finally, we saw with the case of buyers in the chocolate-manufacturing company (chapter 5) that most of the paper files they kept were used *and were usable* only by their owners. This was because the documents in any given file were highly personalized to the owner of the file. The printouts, scribbles, notes, and jottings in each file reflected a buyer's past doings with a particular client. The knowledge about that client and the nature of the relationship was needed to interpret what was in the documents. The importance of this was underlined by the fact that when a buyer was going to be absent, he or she would hand over a file to another buyer to cover for the absence. But before leaving, the buyer would talk through the contents of a file with the covering buyer. This involved giving the replacement buyer up-to-date background information and pointing out the relevance, order, and meaning of the documents in the paper file. It was the necessity of doing this that meant that paper files for current projects were judged by the buyers not to be the kind of "shareable resource" suitable for scanning into a DMS. Too much would need to be added in terms of verbal explanation and know-how about the role of the documents in the past to make electronic sharing practical or possible.

So it follows from all three cases that information is not always ready or suitable for sharing with others. It is not a case of the *medium* preventing the sharing. Rather, the *owners of the documents* prevent the sharing. The use of paper provides a way of doing this. Paper is a local medium, which means that physical possession of a paper artifact is what determines who can access it and who can control it.

Rich Though Inconsistent Indexing of Files   Another finding has to do with the way in which people in different workplaces organize the contents of their paper files. In the organizations we studied there were often attempts by managers to get their employees to standardize their processes. This included the way they put together and organized their files. However, more often than not, we have found that people did not adopt standard practices but rather organized their files they way they found most effective on a case-by-case basis.

For example, in the business processes department of the chocolate-manufacturing company, each project file was completely different from others, not only in terms of its contents but in terms of the way each file was organized. This was because the members of this department tended to have a different file for each project, and no two projects were ever the same. But even in the case of a department with more standardized processes, the supplier department, files were very differently organized depending on which buyer owned them. Not only did no one buyer file documents like another but individual buyers changed the way they filed and categorized their documents from client to client. Documents were often annotated, stapled to other documents, interwoven with printed out e-mails, and ordered and reordered in different ways. Paper supports this kind of inconsistent, changeable, idiosyncratic filing system very well. The only restrictions on how information is categorized and arranged are physical constraints. But these physical and visual cues are rich, varied, and flexible enough to provide huge scope for how documents could be arranged.

Reminding by "Flicking Through"   As it turns out, these features of paper files have a ripple effect in supporting other kinds of behaviors. We found, for example, that buyers who were about to embark on meetings with clients would often pick up a file and quickly flick through the contents to remind themselves of "where they were" in terms of their relationship with that client: what recent correspondence had taken place, what the details of the contract were, and any outstanding issues or problems that needed to be discussed. The physical act of flicking through files, and all the tactile and visual cues that this quickly offered up, turned out to provide good support for this kind of reminding. This tended to happen with files for current projects where no detailed reading was usually required, only quick glances at the collection and organization of the documents.

Reminding Through Physical Presence   Another affordance of paper has to do not with the arrangement of documents *within* a file, but rather with the way the files themselves are arranged. Often, placing files somewhere visible, such as on a chair or a desktop, serves an important role. The mere physical presence of a file serves as a continuous yet relatively unobtrusive reminder of actions that need to be taken or issues to be attended to for current projects.

For example, returning to the case of the buyers, keeping work-in-progress files to hand offered quick access and served to jog the memory for these to-do items. A similar sort of function was served by files that represented upcoming projects or projects just recently dealt with. Here files were often kept more peripherally but still to hand, such as in a desk drawer or in an in tray. Their presence reminded buyers of jobs that needed to be attended to in the near future, or jobs with regard to past but not urgent projects that needed finishing off. Most buyers therefore used the physical arrangement of their paper files in, around, and on top of their immediate desk environment as a way of supporting the flow of work and structuring upcoming tasks.

Portability and Joint Viewing and Markup   For other uses of the paper files, again the affordances of paper come into play in important ways. For example, turning to the buyers again, we found that the portability of paper files meant that they could easily be taken to meetings with clients and that during those meetings documents could easily be gone through and discussed by all concerned. Although buyers had laptops, they explained, going through the materials in meetings with their clients was easier on paper than trying to jointly view a laptop screen. An additional affordance, closely related to this joint viewing, is that documents are also often marked up during meetings, and paper supports this. So although laptops also offered portability, paper files provided a set of affordances that supported what went on during a typical discussion better than the laptop alternative did.

Quick Access to Files   Finally, paper files afford very quick access to information. Paper files for work in progress are usually kept at desk and at hand. This was the case in many of the organizations we looked at. Taking the work of buyers again, files for current clients and work in progress were often kept on the top of the desk or in a briefcase. This way, buyers could find answers to questions quickly when clients or co-workers phoned, a sign, in turn, of their expertise with respect to a particular client relationship. Quick access was possible with the paper files not only because they were immediately to hand but also because, as we said before, their owners were very familiar with their contents. This familiarity was further supported by the physical and visual cues used in the organization of the contents of each file.

Hot, Warm, and Cold Files   So paper files are valuable in supporting a range of activities. What is interesting is that all the affordances we have discovered are those that bring benefits in terms of the use of the documents that people use to support work in progress. In other words, paper files bring a range of advantages when they embody a working set of documents that is kept to hand, arranged on the desktop, flicked through, carried to meetings, marked up, and so on. These are the documents we have called hot and warm. Such documents tend to be highly personalized in terms of content and organization, and in terms of the fact that they are not intended for sharing with others.

We can contrast this with what happens with the documents and files that we call cold. These are the dusty archives, the files and documents that represent projects completed in the past. Many of them are the products of people who have long since moved on. Often these stacks of documents are archived and never used again, eventually occupying off-site storage facilities because organizations know they rarely use them but are loathe to ever dispose of them.

For cold files, paper does present a significant problem. Paper simply lacks the affordances necessary to allow organizations to make effective use of them. First and foremost, these kinds of documents accumulate steadily and take up a huge amount of space. The volume of information alone makes them difficult to search through. This is a problem for the owners of files in that, through sheer passage of time, just what is there and where it is filed soon becomes a distant memory. It is perhaps more of a problem for people who inherit these large paper collections. These files may be quite meaningless to their new owners. This problem is often made worse by the fact that there is usually no one around to interpret the files because those who originally owned them have moved on. Added to this, files quickly lose their relevance because times change and organizational contexts change. This is not just a problem for paper files, of course, but we have seen how paper files in particular often contain a large amount of personalized information that is in itself difficult for an outsider to interpret. A final problem is for people who might be potential customers for these files but who have no way of knowing that important nuggets of information may exist somewhere buried deep in a paper archive. Paper simply does not afford widespread awareness and access for a large audience of potential consumers. There are many ways, then, in which paper is an outdated, unsuitable technology for preserving and leveraging knowledge of the past.

The Affordances of a Digital Document Management System

If paper is the medium that does little to revive the information organizations keep in cold storage, digital DMSs offer affordances that do provide the possibility of unleashing its potential.

Storing Large Amounts of Information in a Small Space   The most obvious attractive property of DMSs is that they require a relatively small amount of physical space for storing huge amounts of information. As we outlined in chapter 2, the gap between digital and paper storage continues to widen with advances in digital storage capacity. Given that much of the paper that is stored consists of old files that are infrequently used, the cost in terms of real estate and upkeep of large paper collections is hard for most organizations to justify.

Widespread Access to Information Stores   DMSs offer access to vast stores of information for a potentially huge audience. Documents that might be of relevance to others can therefore achieve a much bigger distribution and reach a much wider audience than ever before. Access also works both ways, so that the more consumers there are for information, the more contributors to that information there can be. The potential for preserving knowledge is therefore greatly enhanced by a DMS.

Remote Access to Information Stores   A related aspect of this is that use of a DMS means that the potential audience is more or less free of both geographical (and temporal) constraints. This essentially means that once a document is submitted to a DMS, its owner is taken out of the loop. Unlike a paper document, which might be kept in an owner's filing cabinet, the information is now accessible anywhere, anytime, by anyone authorized to use the system. The owner is therefore no longer the gatekeeper or controller of access. All information is now more or less published to those eligible to use the system.

Fast, Exhaustive Searching of Information Stores   Not only can users gain access to huge stores of information, they also have a number of powerful tools available to help them search that information. Automatic search facilities like full-text keyword searches are the most common, allowing users to apply a set of criteria to the entire contents of a given database. Many DMSs also provide software to automatically extract features from scanned documents, such as its form or various aspects of its contents, to enable these searches to occur. These tools support goal-directed searching very well: the kind of searching people do when they know what they are after. For example, it would enable us to search a database for anything containing the keywords "paperless office." Note that this kind of searching is very different from what we might call "browsing." By browsing we mean not goal-directed searching but what people do when they want to familiarize themselves with what's in a database or a folder: the quick, almost random scanning of contents, and the often serendipitous discovery of information.

Flexible, Systematic Viewing and Sorting   Other tools that allow DMS users to explore the contents of a database are viewing and sorting tools. These allow users to choose from among a set of different criteria (e.g., by name, by date, by document type) to view or sort information systematically and exhaustively. These tools are flexible in that documents can be organized and reorganized effortlessly, changing the way in which the documents are laid out or presented, but they are systematic in that they are organized along a fixed set of criteria.

Quick Links to Related Materials   Another affordance of DMSs is the ability to electronically access one document through another with the use of hyperlinks. This way of moving through an informational space and discovering other documents of potential relevance involves much less effort than in the paper world, where, even in libraries, readers must spend time and effort tracking down other related sources of information.

Dynamically Updating or Modifying Content   In addition to being able to navigate through a database and view it in different ways, a final important property of a DMS is that its contents can be easily changed or updated. For consumers of information this means that DMSs can be the place where one can find the latest version of a particular document or piece of information. Consumers can also draw together and reuse documents or parts of documents and customize them for their own purposes. For contributors to a database this means that a DMS is an ideal place to post documents that are regularly subject to change, such as project proposals, schedules, and the like.

All these affordances provide a good foundation for the development of systems that not only can help preserve the knowledge in an organization but can help people access and reuse that knowledge. However, these features alone do not guarantee effective use of an organization's cold archives.

Lessons for Design

Now is the time to ask what we can say about new directions for document management technologies by studying the use of paper. We can do this by reflecting on what we have said so far about the affordances of paper and the affordances of DMSs. We have seen, for example, that the affordances of paper are ideally suited to supporting the way in which people use documents for work in progress: that is, for hot and warm files. When we look at the digital alternatives, we have seen that they are much more poorly suited to such document interactions, though they provide better affordances for cold files. In other words, as table 6.2 shows in summary, they are not parallel or equivalent.

This leads to a set of requirements that takes the use of these different kinds of files and documents into account.

Table 6.2
The Affordances of Paper and DMSs for Document Sharing and Management

---

Affordances of Paper
Controlling access until information is "ready"
Rich though inconsistent indexing of files
Reminding by "flicking through"
Reminding through physical presence
Portability of files for meetings
Jointly viewing and marking up while in discussion
Quick access to work-in-progress files

Affordances of DMSs
Storing large amounts of information in a small place
Widespread access to information store
Remote access to information store
Fast exhaustive searching of information store
Flexible, systematic viewing and sorting
Quick links to related materials
Dynamically updating or modifying content

Support for Different Kinds of Documents   With regard to the shareability of information, many DMSs provide no clear distinction between documents that are personal resources and those intended to be shared resources. This is a problem because, as we have seen, many of the documents we use in our work are personal tools, often being the products of work in progress. By this we mean that it often takes work to make a document shareable by anyone else. Consider how easy it is to decipher one's own notes from a recent meeting versus looking at someone else's notes for a meeting you were not party to. Making documents understandable to others often means one has to polish them, add some context by way of background, and so on. We often want to store documents without having to do this extra work, whereas at other times we want to deliberately make these documents shareable by our immediate work group, a larger part of the organization, or even more broadly. The design of DMSs should allow users to easily make these distinctions in "degree of shareability."

Findings such as these point out that rather than viewing the collection of documents within an organization as one pool of knowledge to which people need increased access, there are, very generally speaking, three ways of characterizing documents. Some documents are really best suited only for personal use. Here we do not mean that they are necessarily "private" documents, containing sensitive or secret information. Rather, many of the documents that people keep are only understandable by the people who own or create them. It is not clear that others could leverage information from such documents however much they wanted to. Such documents could be misinterpreted, especially if they were mistaken for being "shareable" when in fact they were not intended to be. The implication is that these kinds of documents are simply not suitable for a DMS, or at least should be marked in some way as work in progress, as the kind of hot and warm documents unsuited for widespread sharing.

The next category refers to documents that might be used at a work group level. Many such documents will also be work in progress, but the difference here is that they may reflect collaborative work in progress that others need access to because they are involved in the process. So they are work in progress but not personalized. Here the success of sharing such documents depends on the fact that the people who share know each other, or at least know something about the jobs and processes that others are involved in. Thus, a flipchart from a meeting is shareable if one was in the meeting in which it was produced (figure 6.4). The point here is that people would be unlikely to understand the markings on the flipchart unless they knew the topic of the meeting, the status of the projects related to the meeting, and who else was involved in the meeting. Similarly, action plans may only be relevant to the team who needs to orient to that plan, and they may be largely uninteresting to people who work outside of the remit of the plan. The implication here is that DMSs need to be designed so that work group–related documents are seen as fundamentally different from personalized documents.

Finally, there are documents that are shareable by the organization at large, and it is here that a DMS may have the most significant impact. Finalized documents are the obvious candidates, as are companywide resources such as travel information, forms, organizational charts, and so on. These kinds of documents often have to be prepared specially prior to being made available for remote access and wide distribution. This usually involves some overhead for the person who creates or owns the document.

Figure 6.4
The common output of meetings: lots of flipchart paper.

These are the kinds of key differences we find in documents in organizational life, yet many kinds of DMSs do not recognize such distinctions. For example, in the police database we discussed earlier, entering a document into the system automatically meant it was accessible to all who were authorized to use that system. Hence paper served as a workaround to this design flaw. It has to be said that many DMSs do provide features that allow users to restrict access to certain folders, and others allow users to prevent wider access to their own personal resources. Indeed, in most organizations that have implemented DMSs, such a distinction tends to emerge quite naturally, with some kinds of folders being used as holders of work group or organizational documents and others used as places where personal work is filed. But, ironically, even in the face of these user-led trends, pressure in the opposite direction often comes from the DMS implementers, who claim that the "full benefits" of a DMS can only be realized if any and all information is made accessible to everyone.

The point we want to make here is not about access to information and whether systems should be completely open but about how the design of

DMSs needs to be based on a recognition that all documents are not alike. One benefit of this would be that those who implement such systems— whether they be information technology managers or others—would not insist on achieving an unobtainable ideal: universal access. A DMS should be based on a recognition that because documents differ in the extent to which they are intended for sharing or not, their use, provenance, and meaning also differ. Consequently, a priority for DMS designers is to pro- vide users with quick and easy ways to clearly demarcate between the per- sonal documents still part of work in progress, the documents that are also work in progress but shareable across a work group, and the documents that are fully shareable across an organization at large. Designers of DMSs therefore need to give some thought to how users could label or organize their files in such a way as to reflect the intended audience of a document. For example, all documents might, by default, be labeled "personal work in progress" unless users chose to label them "work group document" or as suitable for publishing in the company library.

Better Support for Hot and Warm Documents   These suggestions are perhaps the most obvious ones that can be made about DMSs. But there are more important yet closely related requirements that follow from this, which would require designers to think more carefully about their solu- tions. It is not just a case of making distinctions between these three broad groups of documents visually. As we have seen, work-in-progress docu- ments, whether personal or for the work group, are used differently from documents that are finished and filed away. This is a contrast between how hot and cold documents are interacted with. Users not only need to be able to tell the difference at a glance, but different features and tools should be associated with these different classes of documents.

Consider the hot and warm documents first, particularly personal work- in-progress documents that usually are kept in paper form. One of the fea- tures that paper supports here is a rich set of physical and visual features that are used in filing and indexing. Paper files are constituted differently from person to person and from file to file. They make use of many features of paper to convey meaning. First, the actual drawing together of a set of materials in a paper folder indicates the materials are related, but then the way the materials are ordered and interwoven as well as the way pieces of paper are annotated, attached one to another, have Post-it notes appended, and so on, all play important roles. Perhaps most important is that so much information can be seen at a glance, or at least with a quick riffle through a file. As such, paper folders are good tools for supporting *browsing* or *reminding*.

Compare this to the way users are forced to view the contents of most electronic folders in a DMS. Open up a folder and usually all that is available is a document title and some indication of the kind of document it might be (a presentation versus a word-processing file, for example). The actual contents of a document are more or less hidden from view. There are no cues to indicate whether a document might be marked up, whether it contains graphics or mostly text, whether it is long or short. Though there are some ways of finding this out with various DMSs, typically users have to browse through a set of documents and laboriously open and then close document after document.

The way the documents are laid out also offers minimal cues about what the documents are and how they are related to one another. In most DMSs, users cannot virtually staple one document to another, add Post-it notes, or otherwise make one document look distinct from another, though some DMSs do offer views of "as scanned" versions of files that may include such annotations. Techniques for laying out files within a folder are also limited, which means that the contents in any one folder do not, at a glance, look much different from those in another. We have seen in the paper world that such properties can make paper folders look very distinct, both from the outside and the inside. The point here is not that the digital world needs to mimic the paper world but that electronic filing techniques could make use of a much richer set of visual cues (such as thumbnails) and a much looser style of organization to support reminding and browsing. Such visual cues and loose structuring are intrinsic to how individuals use personal hot and warm files. The same concerns are also applicable when hot and warm files are used by a work group, that is to say, as part of a set of shared processes where the documents in question are part of work in progress. Here, too, the kinds of variegated and subtle cues that can enable users to understand the exact nature of a document and its relation to other documents and activities are often visual and loosely structured, and again it is this that needs to be supported.

Other requirements we have seen for personal hot and warm files include quick access, portability, and the ability to jointly view and mark up documents. The issue of quick access is perhaps the first and foremost of these in that it is not simply a question of the response time of the system, although this is an important if not crucial factor and one that troubled many of the people we interviewed about DMSs. Quick access means being able to find information in a hurry and then being able to use it in appropriate ways: for example, to take to meetings, and to work through, annotating as appropriate with co-workers. Speed of access is partly supported by the rich array of cues in paper folders that we have just described. Fast system response time coupled with better support for browsing through documents will help in those situations where people need to have information quickly to hand.

This leaves requirements that are mainly to do with meeting support and the kinds of activities people engage in when they are away from their desks or even their offices. As we have seen, most people take paper documents with them because of the affordances they offer in discussion or meeting situations. So, though laptops are available and indeed are sometimes used as part of a meeting, paper still provides the key resource or tool. One of the main reasons why laptops fail to offer an effective alternative to paper in such situations is that they make it difficult to jointly view documents, especially for large groups. Of course, laptops are often hooked up to projection hardware for presentations, but such projection technology is inappropriate for many kinds of focused, informal, and interactive discussions people have at work. It is not only the viewing of documents that is at issue: laptops do not adequately support navigation through documents nor collaborative mark-up and annotation.

What this suggests is that designers of DMSs need to recognize that there is a flow of documents in and out of the system when they are taken away to meetings, and that those documents come back marked up. For this flow to happen entirely in the digital world, documents from a DMS need to be easily copied or accessed through a portable device designed with meeting support and work away from the desk in mind. Such devices need to support pen input for mark-up. They also need to allow joint viewing of documents. Once again, this does not need to be accomplished by emulating how this is done with paper. A paper-based model would point to the viewing of documents by two or more people looking at a single LCD screen, but most LCD screens are notoriously bad for reading from a range of viewing angles. Joint viewing can be achieved, however, through multiple devices that synchronize viewing, or through the use of projection screens. Using bluetooth or infrared capabilities, users could "beam" documents to one another to achieve sharing for the purpose of discussion, for example.

Just as a DMS needs to support the taking away of documents, so it needs to consider those that are brought back. A key issue here is that most of these documents will be modified versions of the documents taken away. They may now contain annotations or small changes to the underlying texts and may be accompanied by other related documents acquired while the worker was mobile. The DMS needs features and facilities that allow users to easily and quickly incorporate and update these hot documents back into their own collections.

Support for Cold Document Archives   These, then, are some ways in which people's use of hot and warm documents could be better achieved in a DMS. As we have said, though, for many reasons the digital world seems a much better natural fit for supporting the storage and archiving of cold documents. Users can choose from a powerful set of tools to allow them to access, search, and reuse information that has been archived. But, here again, designers of DMSs can learn from the case of paper to do this job better than they currently do.

As we have pointed out, one of the side effects of digital rather than paper archiving is to take document owners out of the loop. In other words, a DMS allows access to documents without the involvement of an individual owner or human gatekeeper. This is not necessarily a good thing. We have found in all our studies of documents that people almost always have a story to tell about the documents they own. They might tell us why a certain document is important or how it reflects a bit of the company's history. They might tell us where they got a document, who created it, and why. They might give us a quick overview of what's in a document and direct us toward the sections to read and those we can skip.

Now take those conversations away, and all you have is the documents. This would not be a problem if only documents spoke for themselves. But we have seen that many of the documents people use on a day-to-day basis are largely unintelligible to anyone but their owners. The truth is that even documents that are intended to be shareable and understood by a larger audience differ in the degree to which they truly are stand-alone objects. Part of the problem here is that circumstances and organizational contexts change. Reports can therefore refer to projects that may no longer exist. Articles can make reference to people who are no longer with the company. Catch phrases and acronyms come and go.

In the digital world, the stories disappear because the owners disappear. And there is another problem: in the paper world, if there is no one there to tell the story, people try to reconstruct it by identifying the relation between documents on the basis of their own experience. Their experience cannot enable them to completely rebuild the story, of course, but it does enable them to at least construct a rough version. This is one of the reasons that "old hands" in a workplace can be so valuable: they can interpret files and documents from the past in ways that newcomers cannot.

Putting aside the importance of "old hands," one of the affordances of a DMS is something that can undermine attempts to reconstruct the story surrounding filed documents. A DMS allows users to view and reorganize documents in many different ways, and only a few of these—perhaps only one—actually reflect the ways in which those files were originally related to one another by the people who created or owned them. Consequently, the very choice that a DMS provides may not in the final analysis aid the user in understanding these important interrelations, those interrelations that help tell the story of what documents mean and how they fit into a larger organizational context. If this happens, users may find themselves in the situation of treasure hunters whose map—provided in this case by the DMS—does not in fact help them get to the treasure.

The issue for designers, then, is how to indicate the value of a document to an organization by indicating what the *story* about the document might be. This story will be made up of common elements, including information about who created it, who owned it, how it was used, why it was created, and why it was kept. The story may be thought of as a map of those relations.

Whatever solution the designers come up with, it must obviously impose only a small overhead on its users. What is also certain is that there will be two elements to that solution. The first involves providing various kinds of annotations for archived documents, including text-based notes, voice, and video. It is quite straightforward to associate such elements within a database, the task simply being one of linking so-called tags identifying elements. It does not matter whether those elements are text, image, video, or hybrids of these. Once this is done, a DMS could present to a user an image of a document, for example, concurrent with a voiceover that talks about that document.

The second element will be much more difficult to provide. These particular understandings need to be placed within a larger frame of reference: the story as a whole. To go back to our treasure map metaphor, if the multimedia annotations provide information about any particular document, they may be thought of as information about any particular place on a map. What is required is the information that puts those places together on a map as a whole. This is where the difficulty resides. Consider how buyers ran through their files. They moved their hands through a file and pulled out first this and then that piece of paper; they pointed at this paragraph and those annotations while telling a story that provided an overall rationale for their activity. In other words, buyers not only referred to various parts of a document in nonsequential ways but also juxtaposed sections of more than one document.

One way of thinking about how to provide this in a digital context would be to explore notions of how to capture and preserve narratives in relation to a collection of documents. In other words, we can ask what kinds of technological interfaces to a DMS might allow the owners of documents to tell the stories associated with their collections in a way that is at once easy for them and that allows future users to "play back" these stories in such a way that they can see the documents referred to and hear the voiceover stories associated with them. What comes to mind are some of the innovative approaches to interaction with digital and paper documents that involve over-the-desk scanning of paper documents as well as over-the-desk projection of digital documents through a desktop camera and projector mounted over the physical desktop.[8] This sort of system also allows the capture of marks made both to paper and to virtual copies of documents as well as the capture of hand movements over documents. Not only can they be captured but they can be replayed later on. Such systems could be made part of an interface to a DMS, and doing so would mean that the desktop activities of people in relation to their documents (activities that may combine the hands and the eye, virtual and paper documents) could be captured in a way that places only a small burden on the user. All that would be required is that users turn on the system to provide a final run-through of their document collections. Indeed, this could be the last task they were asked to do before they moved on. This could then be replayed in the future whenever any one wanted to reuse those documents. This scenario is not so far-fetched. Indeed, the technology already exists to do it. All that is needed is for this kind of system to be optimized and modified as an interface to a document archiving and management system.

Conclusion

In our discussion of the future of reading, we noted that Xerox had researched ways of altering some of the fundamental assumptions that underscore reading. Similarly, what we are suggesting here is a wholly new way of approaching how a DMS might provide the tools that users need. One such set of tools involves replicating the kinds of run-throughs that individuals give their colleagues when they are handing over hot and warm files for an anticipated absence. The hope is that these narratives will then confer value onto files that ordinarily would lose their value with the passing of time and after they had been moved off to cold storage.

   Coming up with these sorts of solutions as well as some of the less radical design requirements has resulted from investigation of how the affordances for interaction provided by paper can be embodied in new technologies. Here we have tried to provide some examples both in the context of digital reading devices and DMSs. But this is not the only way of approaching the problem of how to design for the future. An alternative approach is to accept the usefulness of paper as one kind of technology and attempt to develop ways of integrating that technology with another, namely, electronic. Examples here include glyphs (fancy bar codes) and associated smart paper technologies that allow users to link paper documents, through scanning, with data in the digital world. The possible system we describe for the DMS that incorporates over-the-desk scanning and projection equally involves both paper and digital technologies. Various systems for remote collaboration over paper via video connections have also been developed (mainly in the research world). This approach broadens the options for users and helps to surmount some of the technical obstacles that often force people to choose between one kind of medium and another.

Alongside considerations of aspects of the design of technology, the examples taken from the settings we have described in this chapter also make the point that organizational work processes and the use of paper have often if not always coevolved (as they have with a host of other mundane technologies such as files and filing cabinets). Consequently—an important point on which we conclude this chapter—attempts to alter the role of paper or to replace paper in those processes will affect the organization in more far-reaching ways than an examination of only the local aspects of interaction would reveal. As we have noted, it is therefore a step not to be undertaken lightly. In this chapter, we have focused on two tasks in which paper has a key role: reading and filing. There are many other tasks in which paper has a role in organizational life. Whatever that role, the relation between that paper and the organizational processes it is part of need to be carefully specified before attempts to do away with paper are made. It is only by better understanding what paper currently does, much in the way we have attempted to do here, that the future evolution of work processes and supporting technologies can be undertaken. Such a study may show that certain processes will need to retain the use of paper, at least for the foreseeable future. Other processes may need to be redesigned in ways that gradually reduce the need for paper, perhaps by introducing new technological alternatives that preserve some of the affordances of paper important for those processes, perhaps by changing the processes themselves. Whatever is the case, the point needs to be made clear: without paper, organizations would be very different places than they are now. But to make sure that organizations reach into the future in ways that ensure that they are more efficient rather than less, they need to recognize what is good about the present as well as what is bad. In this chapter, we have focused on what paper is good for and suggested that some of these properties, some of these affordances, can be designed into digital alternatives. These in turn can be combined with the affordances that digital technologies provide to create hybrids that are at once powerful and familiar.

The Future of Paper

Offices have changed a great deal over the past century. Some of these changes have been brought about by apparently quite ordinary technology. The invention of the vertical filing cabinet, for example, radically expanded the amount of information that could be stored in any one office, contributing to the emergence of truly distributed organizations.[1] The telephone was, of course, another revolutionary technology; the PC a more recent driver of change.[2] Yet throughout these developments paper has stubbornly remained a key tool in office life. So, what will the office of the future look like? Will it be radically different and wholly paperless? Or will it be the reverse, perhaps all too familiar, filled with difficult-to-use technologies but still burdened with excesses of paper?

We think that the office of the future will be a very different place than it is today. New technologies will continue to be developed and will find their own niche in the office of the future. Some will have a huge effect; others will have very little. Similarly, the role of paper will continue to evolve and change. In some arenas it will disappear; in others it will persist or even assume more importance. There will be changes, too, in work practices and organizational processes, and these will leverage the opportunities innovative technologies can provide. Finally, there will continue to be changes in the way office spaces are used, in the patterns of work, and in where and when people do their work. This will spark new technologies and ways of working as well as more fundamentally changing our concept of what an office is.

But what can we say more specifically about the role of paper in the office of the future? It is at this point that we revisit the questions we posed at the beginning of this book: How much paper will there be in the office of the future? Is a mix of paper and digital technologies inevitable? What will the role of paper be in five, ten, or twenty years? As we said at the outset of the book, rather than resort to trend analyses, we have tried to answer such questions by looking at the underlying reasons why people continue to use paper in the face of digital technologies. To do this we have covered many different aspects of paper use and looked at many different kinds of workplaces. What we found is that there are three kinds of reasons that people stick with paper despite the burgeoning of digital devices populating today's modern offices:

1. *The coevolution of paper and work practices.*   Paper and work practices have coevolved over the years, and changing these long-standing work patterns within existing social, technological, and cultural infrastructures is difficult.

2. *The need for better design of digital alternatives.*   Many digital alternatives to paper are inadequately designed for the tasks at hand and for accomplishing the goals people are trying to achieve. Thus, paper often does the job better and enables people to work around the problems posed by technological alternatives (many of which were originally introduced to replace paper).

3. *The affordances of paper.*   Paper has particular affordances that make it the best choice for some tasks at hand and that will likely continue to make it the preferred medium for certain work tasks in the foreseeable future.

Each of these reasons allows us to say something more substantial about the status of paper in the office of the future. Although it is very difficult to pinpoint *when* changes will occur, what we have discovered about paper use lets us say something about *what kinds* of changes we expect and what *preconditions* are necessary before these changes can take place.

Coevolution of Paper and Work Practices

Much of this book has been about the difficulties organizations have in bringing about change in a desired direction. One or two of the workplaces we have looked at have undertaken change very effectively; but most have found the transformations much slower to effect than they had expected. Most have also found the process a painful one. Those instigating movements toward a paperless office have often found themselves disappointed when expectations have fallen short. Those affected by these initiatives have, at best, found their work compromised and, at worst, seen the efficiency, productivity, and even safety of their existing processes undermined.

Looking at so many different work settings allows us to point to two important issues here, corresponding to two of the major themes we have explored in this book, namely, (1) that getting rid of paper often assumes a symbolic role in office life, one that can get in the way of understanding the real underlying problems that may exist; and (2) that the role of paper in office life needs to be understood as having coevolved with work practices and thus as being hard to disentangle and alter.

Both issues are about complexities and interdependencies. To unravel them, and to make the path to change a smoother one, fortunately we have seen that there are practical steps that organizations can take:

• *Dispel the myths.*   First and most important, some of the myths surrounding the office of the future need to be dispelled. The idea that there are always benefits to going paperless is one such myth. There need to be clear-cut reasons for making changes, based on a good understanding of the existing social, physical, and technological infrastructures already in place in any given work setting. Change for the sake of change is hugely problematic. Going paperless for the sake of "out with the old, in with the new" is destined to end in failure.

• *Understand the broader picture.*   Second, there needs to be better recognition that office environments are not just about old and new technologies such as paper and desktop computers. Of central importance here is that office environments revolve around people and the ways people share informational artifacts and know-how. This includes the interdependencies of different forms of information, one supporting the use of another, and so on. Offices are ecologies, and when well designed and maintained, they are ecologies that thrive, allowing people to work more effectively both within their confines and elsewhere (at home or on the move). Often there is a failure to recognize the importance of looking at this broader picture when trying to select the technologies and design the organizational processes of the office of the future.

Before we look at what this means for the office of the future, let us say more about what we mean by the broader picture. Here it is helpful to revisit what an office is and what it consists of.

What Is an Office?

Throughout this book we have looked at various elements of office environments, though, of course, with a bias toward looking at paper. In our approach, we have attempted to look at the bigger picture—to look not only at the specific ways in which office workers use the tools they have to hand and at the tasks they do but also to consider how these practices have come to be, how they fit into the larger social and cultural milieu, and what these practices mean to people. This approach contrasts with much of the work on office and factory life that took place in the early and middle twentieth century. This work was focused on measuring and improving the performance of specific tasks.[3] Since then, other people have looked at offices in a much more holistic way, recognizing that offices are in fact complex systems, involving much more than simple processes with inputs and outputs.[4] They are made up of social fabrics and subtle arrays of tools and technologies. They are as much anthropological phenomena as they are cognitive, and though they are based on processes and rules, they are pervaded by moral codes.[5]

In various ways, all this research has shown that effective offices of the present day are not simply a function of the way an office environment is laid out or the various information tools and technologies in the office (whether they be paper or digital media). Nor are they simply a function of the people who populate an office or the work processes they engage in. They are a product of the *interaction* of these things. There are many ways in which this is so, but here we want to highlight three key concepts that help to explain how.

Information Ecologies   This is a term for the way different forms of information are made useful by their interdependence with other forms of information. By way of a simple example, consider how it is that a Post-it note may have no value in itself until it is attached to another document. Interdependence need not be physically embodied in this way, however. A report may only have meaning through reference to prior reports. Although these reports may be stored in nearby files, the nature of this relation may exist very much in the minds of the people using those reports. Having read the prior reports, they take account of what was said before in order to interpret what is currently before them. The relations between informational resources are therefore often spread out over time. These relations create strands of activity and meaning.

The relations between various kinds of information may not only be of concern to any one person at any one moment in time, however. There is also the relation between the information one person is using and information other people may be using. Here, particular kinds of informational artifacts help create and maintain that interrelation. For instance, all the activities related to some set of reports may be prioritized by a work plan pinned to an office wall. This chart may indicate what needs to be done today and what needs to be done tomorrow, or whose responsibility is one report and whose is another. The meaning of the various reports and all the to-do jobs associated with them are reflected by and given meaning by this chart. At the same time, the chart itself derives meaning from the objects it refers to. Such charts and the documents to which they refer are thus codependent, though they may never be physically attached to each other.

Interactional Affordances of Artifacts   Information ecologies are dependent upon the interactional affordances that office artifacts provide. We have talked a great deal about the affordances of paper. For example, the affordances of a paper report include the fact that it allows flexible navigation and supports the cross- referencing of one report against other reports that may be laid alongside each other on a desk. There are many other interesting artifacts in offices, too, each with its own set of affordances. For example, the affordances of a physical wall chart are that it has a persistent presence and that it is usually of a size and in a location that means it can be seen at a glance anytime by the people who most care about its contents. The affordances of whiteboards support the display of easily modifiable markings to enable participants to sketch out and jointly view the issues at hand for all to see when meetings are held.

Offices are, then, replete with artifacts whose affordances are coopted to help achieve particular ends. Each type of artifact has its own set of affordances, including various interactive, computer-based technologies. An office environment consists of a mix of the advanced and the mundane; of objects that are flexible and portable (such as paper documents); and of environments and objects that are more fixed (such as meeting spaces and the tools and fixtures they contain). An office is a fusion of artifacts, technologies, and spaces.

Communities of Practice   Finally, we turn to the concept of communities of practice. This refers to the informal human networks of information exchange and collaboration that help individuals know what their colleagues are doing and that enable them to collaborate and engage in team work. Communities of practice do this by allowing and indeed ensuring the development of disparate sets of skills that can be marshaled in flexible and typically informal ways to produce successful action. Such communities may spread out well beyond the confines of a particular office—and indeed most often do—and include individuals and groups elsewhere in an organization and even between and across organizations. For example, a community of practice may range from the vast community of researchers that constitute Silicon Valley or the much smaller but equally competitive community of racing car manufacturers in England. People can also be in more than one community.

Crucially, the patterns of collaboration that these communities support are not adequately captured in such things as process charts or formal descriptions of work responsibilities. Communities of practice go beyond and underscore such formal descriptions. The value of a community ranges from providing and propagating anything from arcane kinds of know-how within a group of workers to the support of the most mundane knowledge. For example, membership may provide access to the latest thinking on a subject, made available through coffee room talk, e-mail, or other forms of communication. Membership may also provide resources for an individual to turn to when some technology they depend upon fails. Someone can usually be found who can provide the right assistance to get things working again. This is not always the same person, with one or two people being good at some kinds of problems and others being expert at other sorts of problems. This is one of the reasons that communities of practice take time to develop and one of the reasons why their dissolution can be so consequential for organizations.

Revising Our Vision of the Future

These concepts label what interacts in effective office environments. Informational artifacts support and confer meaning on each other; tools and technologies are used as resources whose affordances serve a wide range of purposes; and people are networked, often informally, in ways that leverage their expertise and know-how. It is important to point this out because offices of the future will have to do the same. The only difference is that they will have to do so with a new set of tools and processes in place.

Unfortunately, many visions of the future fail to take these complexities into account. It is quite common, for example, to hear the notion of an office reduced to a flow of information—a description that encompasses only the interfaces necessary to input and output information as well as the tools to manage it. Recently, we have heard many of the mobile equipment manufacturers propagating this kind of view. For instance, we have been told by one company that the digital office of the future will need support for only two basic things: a window on information (something that allows access, manipulation, and storage) and a means of managing personal information while in the office or on the move. As this company saw it, such an office needed only two kinds of technology: powerful laptops (with long-lasting batteries and lightweight, flexible screens) and communications-enabled PDAs (palm-top computers). The laptop would serve as the information window, and the PDA would enable individuals to manage their personal affairs (including address book, diary, expenses) and communication with colleagues. This technology would be enabled by real-time connectivity through a wireless network.

Such a vision (and many others like it) is much too focused, much too simple. An office is not simply an interface to information but, as we have said, an interactive amalgam of information, people, and artifacts working harmoniously together. As such, an effective office consists of a much broader array of tools than a collection of PDAs and laptops could ever provide. It encompasses an information environment that spreads out around the desk and the office walls. It consists of artifacts that support not only an individual's immediate needs but also the needs of teams of people (such as the use of wall charts and whiteboards). It also consists of combinations of tools and artifacts used in conjunction with one another in artful ways. For example, it may mean combining the use of computers to create and manipulate information with the use of paper-based notes, articles, and documents to support cross-referencing and complex navigation. And it involves having access to those who know about work processes and who can assist when they break down (including when technology fails or when new technology is introduced).

So how does change occur? As we have seen, one of the problems of trying to move toward a paperless office is that doing so often involves negatively affecting the interdependencies between various informational artifacts. Sometimes it also undermines the ability of people to work together. It is no wonder that these attempts fail. But because they have failed does not mean change is not possible. It would be wrong to think that these communities of practice, the information ecologies, and the affordances these depend upon cannot be altered. A better view is that they need to be altered and developed in beneficial ways. New interactive technologies can offer better support for work and for office environments. They can do so not by disrupting the already existing information ecologies, but by reinforcing and developing those ecologies.

We have seen that knowledge workers, for instance, interweave their reading, writing, and thinking activities to create information spaces. These can be enhanced by new digital technologies such as e-books, which, if properly designed, will allow those individuals to more effectively get to grips with the information they have at hand. We have seen also how technologies can enhance communities of practice by offering affordances that were not hitherto available. Consider the example of the account managers we discussed in chapter 2. These individuals found that they were able to more effectively participate in their community (focused in the bids and sales department) by accessing online discussion groups and through having daily contact via e-mail. Prior to the introduction of portable equipment and remote access, these individuals were separated from their community when they were out hunting sales prospects. In a sense, they were rather like eighteenth-century sailors who would disappear for weeks on end and then return either with bounty—a sales prospect—or an empty hold when no sales prospects arose. New technologies can therefore effect change for the better even in well-ingrained work practices (although not always in the ways expected).

We have also seen that major overhauls of the work environment, technologies, and processes are possible. A case in point was that of DanTech (chapter 2). But DanTech was special in that the company was at liberty to start from scratch. It was free to undertake extensive changes coinciding with a physical move to new premises. Most workplaces do not have that luxury. All the more reason, then, that they must proceed more incrementally and with caution.

Even so, we found that there were other lessons to be learned from DanTech's success that can be applied equally to organizations undergoing more gradual processes of change:

• *Focusing on the real underlying problems.*   As we have said, visions of the future based on myths need to be set aside in favor of understanding the real underlying problems that an organization may have. Just as paper-based processes may not be the cause of problems for an organization, so, too, new tools and technologies may not provide the solutions. Organizations need to look at the combination of people, artifacts, and processes to assess where problems may lie and how solutions can be implemented. They need to look both broadly and deeply at what exists already.

• *Being willing to revise visions, reassess solutions.*   Once the problems have been assessed, solutions can be ventured. However, solutions needed to be tested and changed if necessary. If they are rejected, there may be good reasons. So organizations need to give people time to adapt, but if they can't, they need to look at changing the solution. Consulting with end users at many points along the way will help with reassessing the solutions. As a result, an organization may have to change what its vision of the future looks like, but it is then likely to achieve a more collectively agreed-upon, realistic one.

• *Managing expectations.*   Implementing successful change is often as much about managing the expectations that people have as it is about changing what they do. In other words, promise a paperless office, and you set yourself up for disappointment and failure. Promise incremental, realistic changes, and goals are more likely to be met, people more likely to be satisfied.

These are some important ways in which organizations can move more effectively and smoothly toward the office of the future, whether or not that means an office with less paper. Key to all of this is that moving forward into the future must take account of the present. Predicting the future is not just about inventing or visualizing it. It is also about shepherding along a process of change and recognizing the importance of the transition.

So, what does this mean for the future of paper in offices? It means that the introduction of new technologies is unlikely, in most environments, to drastically reduce or eliminate paper as quickly or as radically as is often predicted or expected. Rather, in the short term, new technologies will usually *shift* the role of paper rather than *replace* it. Because change is an evolutionary process in complex environments, the new will not replace the old but will coexist with it. In doing so, both new and existing technologies will begin to interact with each other in different ways. These technologies will settle into different roles and niches over time as people make choices about what kinds of tools serve which purposes best. Paper will therefore be with us for some considerable time partly because of the slow pace of change but also because it will be assimilated into newly introduced structures and processes, including those that involve digital technologies.

Designing the Future

So, one main lesson is that there is a need to see the bigger picture. A second main reason why people are reluctant to give up paper is that the technological alternatives they have to hand are simply inferior for the tasks and goals they want to accomplish. Paper is often a fall-back when new technologies go wrong; paper can provide a quick fix; or paper can simply prove itself to be the better tool for the tasks people have before them. Here, then, is a challenge for designers to get new technologies right, to make them much better than they currently are. But we also know that the ways in which people want to accomplish activities are often a direct consequence of having used paper in those activities for so many years. New technologies may then be rejected because the processes they are trying to support have been optimized for use with paper. In a way, designers of new technology face the same conundrum as those who try to envision the office of the future. Does it make sense to invent the future by looking at the present? Does this not anchor us to the old ways of working and steer us toward making only incremental changes? Does this not stifle true creativity?

Again, one of the messages of this book has been that, even with regard to design, we advocate looking at the future very much from consideration of the present. We have argued that treating the current use of paper as a design resource is in fact a radical approach, one that can lead to innovative new designs and even conceptual leaps over what already exists.

Let's look first at traditional approaches to the design of digital technologies. These have largely ignored what role paper may have in the workplace, have been indifferent to the interactional properties paper provides, and have been based on understanding of work activities curiously devoid of the paper-related elements of those activities. It is as if the underlying philosophy is to design away a technology (paper) without reference to what that technology is currently used for. While this is perhaps to exaggerate, it certainly is true to say that within the research and design community, paper has continued to be associated with inefficiency and old practices. One consequence of this is that designers have been somewhat fearful of having anything to do with paper in their work. Something about paper makes them worry that looking at it may result in their not achieving something "radical," something truly "innovative." As we noted in chapter 1, we were certainly subject to such prejudices, encountering surprisingly negative reactions from the technology research community when we started focusing on paper. Fortunately, attitudes within research are now changing, and we are beginning to see more studies that explore why paper is used.

But these prejudices aside, there is a more fundamental reason that looking at paper use has not been a design resource until now: it goes against one of the core beliefs of design philosophy, which says that the future cannot be designed on the basis of the present. The argument goes that new technologies will allow wholly new activities and will transform what is currently done. Since current users may not understand what these changes may be, since they might be unwilling to countenance the full implications of any imposed change in their activities, there is simply no point analyzing their activities. Rather, designers of new technologies should seek to free themselves of conventional ways of thinking and to visualize what *might* be possible, not what is *currently* possible.

There is a lot to be said for this point of view. Visualizing the future through leaps of imagination to whole new environments, new ways of working, and new devices and services can be an inspiring and motivating way forward. But there are also several difficulties with it.

The first is that many designers and developers take no notice of current practices and don't have the foresight to look into entirely new ways of working. Rather, designs are often centered on conventions developed in the digital world, such as the desktop PCs, mouse, keyboard, and windows interfaces they provide. Proffered alternatives to paper may therefore lack imagination and not provide adequate alternative support for the tasks at hand.

A second difficulty is that without looking carefully at how people might make the transition from what they do to what they might do, or without looking at what value users might get from their new designs, designers and developers have to rely to some extent on a "Velcro" model of success. That is, they have to hope that whatever new technology they throw out there into the world will "stick" somewhere. This sometimes works very well, and it often doesn't matter that these new technologies get taken up and achieve success in unexpected ways. But, equally, the majority of these attempts fail, and huge amounts of time and money are often spent marketing the wrong product to the wrong market sector.

Of course, there are ways of relying less on trial and error. For example, new devices, services, or software can be tested against potential end users through iterative user testing either in laboratory settings or in real-world trials. Here, prototype models of new technologies are tried out with people to see how they react and behave in a variety of different tasks and activities. This is a more systematic way of allowing for the development of "far out" possibilities for new designs. This approach, as well as the Velcro approach, are sensible and often result in useful innovation.[6] Designers should, at certain times, concern themselves solely with the future and should disregard the present.

What we are proposing is a way of supplementing these approaches with the possibility of looking at the present as a way of better determining how the future ought to be. As it turns out, when we do this, when we focus on how people currently use paper, we have found time and again that the end result has been design that is *more* original and *less* like conventional digital technology than had we started elsewhere. This is because looking at paper use can inspire new design concepts in a number of ways:

• By looking at *how* people accomplish things in the paper world, new techniques for interaction sometimes emerge that, when translated into the digital world, are in fact quite innovative and unique. For example, looking at how people navigate through paper using two hands and using multiple pieces of paper suggested how we might develop new techniques for two-handed interaction across multiple display screens. These are a far cry from keyboard and mouse input techniques and represent a conceptual leap forward even over pen-based interfaces.

• By looking at the *goals* people are trying to accomplish using paper, ways of accomplishing the same goals in different, non-paper-like ways are often suggested. For example, when we looked at why people hand-deliver paper documents, we found that it was because they often wanted the excuse for social interaction or discussion in the process of exchanging documents. This gave us a number of interesting ideas for building two-way audiovisual links into electronic document exchange services for people who are remote. It also suggested ideas for new kinds of digital devices supporting document exchange and discussion for people who are face-to-face.

• Finally, by studying the *range of activities* people carry out using today's tools and technologies (such as paper), we can begin to understand the great diversity of things that people do, which often get compressed and glossed over by simple terminology. Studying people's behavior often allows us to discern what people do and thus allows us more scope for new invention when we recognize the variety and richness of people's behavior in the real world. For example, studying how people read at work showed the many ways in which people read documents as well as the reasons they did so. This led us to think about different types of reading, which then served as useful leaping-off points for thinking about new design concepts. The result was a set of designs for new e-book devices that look radically different from any of the e-books currently on the market.

This shows that focusing on paper use or, more generally, focusing on the way people currently do things, does not necessarily mean that we need to be tied to the old ways of working. In fact, in our experience, taking inspiration from the way people currently do things has typically allowed us (and the designers we work with) to find new inspiration and develop highly original concepts. This approach has the added advantage of helping to develop new technologies that allow people to leverage the skills they already possess and to draw on the everyday knowledge they already have. In the long run, this leads to interfaces and interaction techniques that are easier for people to understand and learn. It also leads to the provision of technologies that have clear value for people in the activities they already carry out. But more important, this approach can also result in technologies that support people in terms of the goals they need to achieve but that may do this in entirely different ways from how they were achieved with paper. To look at paper use as a design resource, therefore, clearly does not mean doing design through mimicking paper.

Using Paper as a Design Resource

Looking at paper use as a design resource does not necessarily mean that designers and development teams have to work with psychologists, sociologists, or anthropologists. It can be a matter of existing teams learning to take an interest in current practice and carrying out some simple observation of people in workplaces or doing work-related tasks. This has some immediate benefits. First, it forces design teams to ask, For whom are we designing? What environment are we designing for? What current tasks and activities are we hoping to replace or supplement? What goals will our technology help people to achieve? The whole process of design then becomes much more focused on what value designers expect that users will get from the new technology they are proposing.

To fully understand the issues, however, designers can greatly benefit from the insights and expertise that a multidisciplinary team can provide. We have seen that to understand office settings in all their complexity means looking at the cultural and social systems within which people act as well the technological and nontechnological tools that are used in those settings. Here, people with social science backgrounds can bring new perspectives to the design process in terms of understanding the goals that people have in the workplace and the social and cultural infrastructures already in place. By this we don't mean their personal goals as much as those goals intrinsic to the work they are responsible for. These can be determined by the use of naturalistic methods, such as ethnography, as we reported in chapter 3. How people achieve goals can also be studied through more controlled techniques and experimental design, such as the reading studies described in chapter 4. This added knowledge can help make designers and developers more fully aware of the ways in which new technologies are instruments for the achievement of goals in a larger context (in a work situation or within a richer set of tasks) rather than being ends in themselves.

A further point to consider is that the help of multidisciplinary teams can also be very valuable for the purpose of improving the design of existing technologies. Here again, social scientists in field situations can help pinpoint how digital technologies are really used, including the possibility that new technologies are being avoided or that paper is being used as a workaround. From this, improvements to the design of tools (digital or paper) can be suggested. Similarly, laboratory studies may show how paper and online tools support the same task differently, suggest the benefits and drawbacks of different kinds of tools, and outline what design improvements may be made (as we did in chapter 4). Achieving even incremental improvements in much of the technology one finds in the office of today can make a substantial difference to the people who are required to use that technology.

So, what we are suggesting as a way forward for design is a focus on paper use and, more generally, a focus on current practice around paper, bringing to bear social science expertise and methods. This is not to discount the many other ways and means of doing design. But we do believe that design based on a sensitivity to what people do with paper will lead to better, more effective digital technologies in the workplace. We believe that this approach is more likely to lead to paper replacement technologies than a hit-or-miss approach. To be sure, people's needs and goals will evolve, and with the passing of time, the deployment of innovative technology will result in people's doing things differently than they do them now. But it is best not to lose sight of how to design in such a way as to allow a movement between present and future needs.

Where Paper Will Find Its Place

Finally, we turn to the third and final reason that people are reluctant to give up paper. Here it is not so much the case that digital alternatives are poorly designed but rather that paper itself works so well for some of the jobs it is called upon to do. Even as offices and organizations evolve, and even with the best possible design processes, we need to recognize that paper may remain the best tool for some kinds of activities well into the future.

From looking at many different kinds of workplace activities, we can begin to see where paper finds its natural place. We can begin to see where its affordances naturally lend themselves to certain classes of tasks and not to others. This, in turn, leads us to predict that paper will continue to find its place in support of some kinds of tasks but not others.

Why is this so? In chapter 2, we summarized the interactional limitations of paper. We noted that paper requires physical delivery, that it cannot easily be modified, and so on. But we also said that each of these limitations could also be viewed as an affordance. In other words, each property that appears to *detract* from paper's ability to support some kinds of tasks could in fact be seen as *shaping* and *providing support for* other kinds of tasks. An affordance is the obverse of a limitation.

Some key properties of paper are:

• A single sheet is light and physically flexible.
• It is porous, which means that it is markable (absorbs pigment) and that marks are fixed and spatially invariant with respect to the underlying medium.
• It is a tangible, physical object.
• Engagement with paper for the purpose of marking or reading is direct and local. In other words, the medium is immediately responsive to executed actions, and interaction depends on physical copresence.

All of these properties have implications for what actions paper does and does not make possible.

So, for example, the fact that paper is light and physically flexible means that it is ecologically flexible. In other words, it can be easily laid out in the environment, attached to walls and objects, stacked, and overlapped. One could interpret this in the negative sense and point to the fact that paper creates clutter and takes up space. But these properties also mean that paper supports quick, flexible navigation and manipulation: riffling through, place holding with one hand while manipulating with the other, easily and dynamically moving pages in and out of the workspace, placing pages side by side on the desktop, and so on. One of the implications of this is that people who are working together around a desk, for example, can easily perceive what others are doing with documents. Their work activities are rendered visible to others through the physical manipulation of the documents they are working with.

The second property of paper, the fact that paper affords rich variegated marks that are persistent and static, also has a variety of different implications for perception and action in work situations. On the negative side, it means that marks on paper are difficult to modify, transform, or incorporate into other documents. On the positive side, however, we have seen that these properties have many other implications. For example, multiple co-authors on the same document can leave their own idiosyncratic and persistent marks. Thus, any changes made to a text leave a kind of audit trail of actions that contains information about the history of changes on a document, and who made which marks.

The third property of paper, its tangibility and the fact that it has a persistent physical presence, can also be viewed in two ways. On the one hand, as the amount of information within a document increases, so does its physical bulk and its weight. This means that storing paper becomes a problem and carrying and delivering documents requires physical effort. On the other hand, the persistence of paper documents means that leaving them on the desktop creates a physically embodied holding pattern that can reflect the ideas and activities in progress. If you get interrupted or go away, when you return to your office these bits of paper help remind you of where you were in a task. Physical delivery also has benefits in certain situations, for example, hand delivery of paper can be the excuse for social interaction and discussion over documents.

A final set of properties we have mentioned is the fact that paper requires direct physical contact for writing and manipulation of a document, and physical proximity for reading. There are obvious costs and benefits here when compared to digital media. The drawbacks of paper have to do with the inability to remotely access or share documents, as one can do with digital networked document databases. On the other hand, clear benefits have to do with the immediacy and reliability of interaction with paper—a very short response time, no interoperability problems, and so on. More subtle perhaps is the way in which direct interaction with paper, and the ease with which it can be marked up during a conversation, affords effective interaction in the course of a delicate conversation (between doctor and patient, for example). Another implication is the way in which paper is often used as a private holding device for information until it is ready to be shared. The fact that information is on paper means that people can be more in control of who gets access to that document. Temporary documents, notes, work in progress are thus often paper-based until they are ready to be accessed by others in online form.

Digital Versus Paper-Based Tools in the Document Life Cycle

We can see, then, that the properties of paper are exploited in a variety of activities people do in the workplace. The affordances of paper show themselves in many different ways and in many different situations. Just as each limitation of paper can sometimes be seen as an affordance, each limitation of any digital technology can also be construed as an affordance. These, too, are coopted and used to best effect in a wide range of work activities.

This is not to say that people in workplaces ever think *consciously* about the relative merits of the different tools they have to hand for the tasks they have to do. Nonetheless, they do make choices, and they do combine their use of tools to best advantage. For example, people tend to turn to the computer when they need flexible tools for a writing task and turn to paper when they need flexible support for a reading task. Very often, they use both together when doing combined reading and writing tasks. People at some level recognize the affordances of the resources they have to hand and choose the best tools for the particular jobs they need to do. As a result, paper-based tools tend to find their place within some kinds of tasks and not within others. Similarly, certain kinds of digital tools find their own niche for certain kinds of tasks and not others.

This is an important point because it suggests that paper may be ideally suited to certain kinds of tasks and digital technologies to others. This is

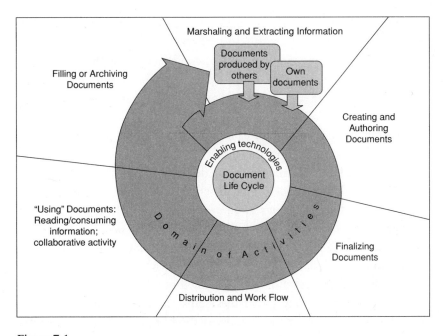

Figure 7.1
The document life cycle.

not to discount the fact that changes in digital technologies will change their role and will affect how paper and new technologies are combined. But given that we have seen many commonalities about the kinds of tasks and activities that paper and digital tools support across a very diverse set of workplaces, and given that these can be linked to some of the underlying properties or affordances of one kind of technology versus another, these are fundamental findings. In particular, it suggests that there might be something fundamental about the kinds of activities that paper supports. If so, then we might expect paper to continue to play a crucial role in these same activities for a long time to come.

So, let's summarize some of the findings with respect to the tasks that digital versus paper technologies seem to support best across different workplaces, looking at it from different aspects of the document life cycle. Figure 7.1 shows some of the major activities that people carry out with documents and information: marshaling and extracting information, creating documents, finalizing and distributing them, and using and archiving them.

While this vastly oversimplifies what people really do with documents, it helps us summarize what we know about how people tend to use paper versus digital tools in each of these phases of document use.

Marshaling and Extracting Information   Digital tools provide powerful tools for quickly searching through vast information repositories and bringing candidate information to the desktop. Other useful affordances include the ability to quickly link to related materials and the ability to view and sort data in various structured ways. As such, digital tools are good at bringing large amounts of information to the attention of the user from what may be unfamiliar repositories of information to allow it to be filtered and extracted.

Paper documents best support browsing through familiar materials. For example, flicking through paper files helps remind owners of their contents. Familiar documents also support thinking and planning activities when users physically lay them out and arrange them in space. This usually involves flexible, unsystematic document organization and reorganization as well as note taking.

Creating and Authoring Documents   Digital tools support the drafting and editing of documents, including the updating, modification, recalculation, and reformatting of text and data. They also support the integration and analysis of data from diverse sources, and the reuse and repurposing of well-defined pieces of documents for new documents.

Paper supports some of the processes prior to writing, such as note taking and making plans for writing. It also supports the cross-referencing of documents during online authoring as an important supporting set of activities. For example, this may mean checking for the consistency of a story across documents or creating a coherent mental picture of what to write by reading across multiple documents.

Finalizing Documents   Digital tools provide the means of formatting, finalizing, and producing professional-looking documents once their contents are determined. Tools such as spelling and grammar checkers also help to automatically check and polish documents.

Printing on paper supports proofreading and getting the sense of the flow of the text. Paper is also the main medium for the reviewing and mark-up of documents by people other than the authors. Here, reviewers may look at documents at various levels, including reviewing contents, syntax and grammar.

Distribution and Work Flow   Digital tools support automated work flow for well-structured, routine processes and transactions. This is turn helps in the standardization of processes. Digital tools also support the fast replication and distribution of information to different people and sites.

Paper also provides a method of achieving effective work flow, but usually it is best when routine processes break down and people need to find a workaround solution. Paper supports delivery of information when social processes are important. For example, hand delivery supports discussion at the point of document delivery.

Reading/Consuming Information   Online tools support the reading of small, well-defined, self-contained pieces of text. They also support viewing and use of multimedia and interactive materials, such as videos, music, and interactive software.

Paper supports reading of longer documents for deep understanding, reading while writing or note taking, reading across multiple documents, and flexible browsing and navigation through documents.

Collaborative Activity   Digital tools (such as groupware and audio-video links) support real-time collaboration for remote conversations and meetings as well as various kinds of asynchronous collaboration (chat rooms, e-mail, document exchange, and so on). They also support the sharing of the same information by more than one person.

Paper tools provide an effective medium for various forms of face-to-face interaction. For example, they provide a flexible mechanism for team coordination in physically shared environments. Paper-based note taking provides support for delicate face-to-face interaction, and paper documents help coordinate and focus discussion in face-to-face meetings.

Filing and Archiving   Digital tools support widespread, remote access to large, shared information repositories. They also support the sharing of the same information by more than one person. These repositories are best for polished, published information (documents that stand alone or are self-explanatory). Digital tools are best for high capacity storage of cold files or information that is not currently in use.

Paper provides a good temporary holding mechanism for knowledge until it is ready to be shared. Paper allows owners to control access to knowledge and to be present when there is a need to explain the relevance or importance of that knowledge. Paper provides good temporary storage for documents with short-term value, for files that have had recent value (warm files), or for files that are currently in use (hot files).

What we can see from all this is that paper tends to find its natural place in workplace activities that are point-of-use activities or that are the kinds of activities we normally think of as key to knowledge work.[7] These are the activities that involve making judgments, solving problems, making sense of information, making plans, or forming mental pictures of information. In other words, these are the activities we have come to think of as getting to grips with information. Paper also finds its place naturally in social processes (especially face-to-face situations), such as those processes that involve discussion, collaborative writing or viewing, and coordinated teamwork. The particular affordances of paper naturally lend themselves to human interaction, either by providing external support for complex internal mental processes or as a tool in support of managing complexities in a collaborative environment.

Digital tools *by contrast* tend to find their natural place for many of the activities *supporting* these point-of-use or knowledge work activities.[8] For example, digital tools offer good support for the accessing and organizing of information prior to its use or prior to the thinking or collaborative processes that need to take place. Digital tools are very well suited to the polishing, finalization, and storage of information after its use. They are also good for managing work flow, distribution, and transactional processes when these are well structured and when these processes go according to plan.

The Role of Paper in the Future
The design of digital tools may eventually be capable of supporting these knowledge work activities much better than they currently do (and especially, as we have argued earlier, if designers look to paper use for guidance). Until such time, paper will maintain its importance in the kinds of roles we have outlined. In other words, it will continue to predominate in activities that involve knowledge work, including browsing through information; reading to make sense of information; organizing, structuring, and reminding of ideas; information integration in support of authoring; and activities that involve showing and demonstrating ideas and actions to others (mark-up of documents, hand delivery, collaborative authoring, and discussion in face-to-face meetings).

Digital technologies, on the other hand, will increasingly take over more of the activities for which electronic media are better suited—those activities in a supporting role for knowledge work: large-scale search and retrieval of information and documents; short messaging for internal/external communications; analysis of data; document production and finalization; processing of business and transactional data; large-scale dissemination and transmission of documents; and long-term, high-capacity storage of cold data and documents. Digital media technologies will also predominate in production and distribution of new kinds of media, such as non linear, searchable documents (dictionaries, reference manuals, encyclopedias), and multimedia genres (videos, music, and interactive multimedia content). We would expect to see, then, that paper is gradually replaced in all these kinds of roles, that it becomes less and less the medium of importance for such things as routine business transactions, intra- and interorganizational communications, large-scale distribution and delivery of documents, and the bulk of storage and archiving of documents in offices.

Note that there are economic, technological, and demographic trends that will reinforce the continuing emergence of paper and digital technologies in these different kinds of roles. For example, in terms of reinforcing paper in its support of knowledge work, consider the following:

• *More and more knowledge workers.* Estimates are that over 30 percent of the U.S. workforce now consists of knowledge workers and that this proportion will continue to grow. More knowledge work means more paper consumed.

• *Mobile working and working from home.*   As people do more work from home and while mobile, the same document is often printed more than once so it can be dealt with in more than one place. Paper now populates not only the workplace but also the home office and the mobile worker's briefcase.

• *Increase in home computer and printer penetration.*   More and more households now own computers and printers as these come down in price. More people also have access to high-quality software to produce their own documents. These trends are now allowing people to easily print at home for many of the same reasons they print in the workplace.

• *Increasing interconnectivity and increases in Web content.*   The power of the Internet and the amount of information available through the Web is transforming the economy. At the same time, it is also allowing an ever-increasing percentage of the population to access vast quantities information from their electronic desktops. More information means increased demand for the means of sorting it out and making sense of it. This is often done through printing on paper.

At the same time, many of these economic, technological, and demographic trends are facilitating the use of electronic tools in the supporting roles for knowledge work we have pointed to:

• *Mobile working and working from home.*   As the number of mobile and homeworkers increases, so too will the need for the infrastructures to support them, such as the need for more reliable networking facilities, better document archiving systems, and better distribution and work flow tools.

• *Increasing interconnectivity and networked computing.*   Advances in networking capabilities, bandwidth, and wireless networking will spur on these changes in infrastructure. At the same time, we will see more demand for tools that can fully make use of these networks.

• *Electronic commerce.*   Data transactions have been handled electronically since the 1960s, but technological trends such as networking, home computer penetration, and the Internet revolution mean a phenomenal surge in business-to-business and business-to-consumer transactional processes.

• *Emerging document exchange standards and interoperable computing.* These changes will help overcome compatibility problems in platforms and applications, facilitating the ease with which workers can access, search, repurpose, and archive information.

• *Better scanning and digital archiving tools.*   Cheaper, better scanning technologies mean that we will in the future be better equipped to deal with the legacy of paper documents we already possess. This means they can be more easily archived in digital form.

All these changes mean not the disappearance of paper in the workplace, but some fundamental changes in its role. We can also see that as digital technologies begin to increasingly inhabit our homes, so too will printing in the home be on the increase.

The Office of the Future

What does this all mean for the future, then? On the one hand, it means that paper manufacturers can take heart: paper consumption will not wane any time soon. On the other hand, it doesn't mean we are looking at a future in which our offices are stuffed with more paper than ever before. In fact, we argue that we are not headed toward offices that *use* less paper but rather toward offices that *keep* less paper. This is because we will continue to need paper for some of the critical work activities we do, but in these roles it will be very much a temporary medium.

So the office worker of the future may well access her information from an electronic database, and she may do this wirelessly from home or from the road. But at the point she needs to deal with it, at the point she needs to read it, reflect on it, and use it in the core of her work, she may well print it. Having done that, she might then turn to digital tools and refer to her paper to create something new in the digital world, or to perform some necessary transactions. Or she might be just as likely to scan what she has been working on to send it electronically elsewhere. Similarly, when a project is finished, she will most likely perform any archiving activities in the digital realm. The paper produced and used in the process may be kept for the duration of the project, but when the project is over and done with, so too will be the paper.

All of this means big changes to offices as we now know them. Look around most offices, and the place where paper affects the office environment most is in the space needed for the filing and archiving of paperwork for past projects, or for the paper forms and stationary needed to carry out routine business processes. Added to this, consider the warehouses full of paper archives that many organizations need to maintain. When offices begin to keep less paper, their landscapes, costs, and work processes will also be significantly altered.

What this also means is that the place of technology in the office of the future will evolve and develop in certain ways. There will not be fewer printers, for example, but more of them. In the future they will sit on everyone's desktop. They will be the personal device for transforming information into the only form usable to carry out some key activities. In many ways, this is trend that is already observable, though the reasons for it have not been properly understood. There will be some changes, also, in the design of printers, particularly in the methods used to deliver print jobs given the ongoing emergence of air-based networks and protocols, for example. But essentially printers will remain a fairly stable technology subject to incremental improvements.

The scanner will be a second key tool, becoming a vital part of the personal technology of the office, being the route into the digital archives for preserving and making accessible those bits of paper that have been read and marked up in the process of knowledge work. Scanners, like printers, are becoming increasingly ubiquitous, although unlike printers their design is likely to change substantially. Innovations will allow richer ways of capturing documents, for instance, and this will include over-the-desk scanning. Here the user will be able to select specific elements of paper-based materials to scan, as well as using scanning as a way of interacting with digital documents in real time. Such applications are already in the marketplace, though they have yet to reach a mass market.

Both scanning and printing technologies are, of course, familiar technologies, while some of the other technologies we have described, such as multiscreen reading devices, have yet to reach beyond the prototype stage. Once technologies become familiar, they become subject to the symbolic world of offices. It was with this topic that we commenced our empirical discussions. We saw in chapter 2, for example, that many organizations think of scanners as a technology that can help do away with paper and printers, especially desktop printers, as technologies that are encouraging people to print too much. According to this view, printers and scanners are battling over paperlessness. But we saw that such symbolic meanings are profoundly wrong. Printers, scanners, and paper are not competitors; they are part of the required tool set of any office, supporting each other in performing distinct roles within the document life cycle.

And yet symbols—whether they are right or wrong—are important. It is symbols that motivate people; it is symbols that are used to measure change, success, and failure. The lab we discussed in chapter 2 hid paper documents from the eyes of visitors so as to be seen to be reaching into the future; it was having paper documents at hand that enabled police officers to appear competent when meeting with the public. Thus, symbols are complex and often full of paradox. Even the most mundane artifacts get laden with meaning.

Consider the lowly wastebasket. In the past, a wastebasket stuffed to the brim with paper could symbolize inefficiency and an organization looking to the past rather than the future. One of the by-products of paperlessness would have been the disappearance of wastebaskets and hence the loss of that symbolic meaning. But now it should be clear that wastebaskets will have an even more important role in the future. According to the vision we have outlined, a full bin will reflect the fact people are working effectively because they are using paper at various stages in the document life cycle, particularly in the knowledge-intensive stages. As they move on to other stages later in the life cycle, the role of paper diminishes. At this point they will no longer need it, and it will become the detritus of their work.

This has some delightful paradoxes for the symbolic meaning of full wastebaskets. It means that if wastebaskets never get filled up with paper, then the kinds of temporary uses that we have identified as essential to various kinds of knowledge-based activities are not being done. Or, if such activities are being undertaken, then the staff in question is not using the best medium for the job at hand. In this situation, office managers need to worry about how to get their staff to use more paper. Hence the symbolic meaning of the wastebasket could be reversed. If in the past a full bin was an indication of waste and inefficiency, in the future it will be the empty one that makes people worry.

Of course, full bins and empty bins are at opposite ends of a continuum, and it will almost certainly be the case that the norm will be somewhere in between. But what is important to recognize is that the role of paper as a temporary medium will be a vital part of offices. The symbolic meaning of wastebaskets is merely a playful example illustrative of the reasons that this will be so. Needless to say, our intentions in this book have been altogether more serious. We have wanted to explain, through empirical evidence and research, why this vision of the future should not dismay technologists and organizational managers or the people who actually work in offices. The paperless office is a myth not because people fail to achieve their goals, but because they know too well that their goals cannot be achieved without paper. This held true over thirty years ago when the idea of the paperless office first gained some prominence, and it holds true today at the start of the twenty-first century. We hope to have shown that it will hold true for many years to come.

Notes

Chapter 1

1. "The Office of the Future" (1975).

2. D. A. Norman, *The Invisible Computer*, 7–13. For more detail, see L. Gitelman, *Scripts, Grooves, and Writing Machines*, 21–27.

3. V. Bush, "As We May Think" (1945). An excerpt from this article can be found in M. Stefik's *Internet Dreams*, 15–22; this quotation is from p. 17.

4. J. C. R. Licklider, *Libraries of the Future*, 5.

5. For a full account of the story, see D. K. Smith and R. C. Alexander, *Fumbling the Future*.

6. *Pulp & Paper International* (July 2000).

7. As reported in G. Rifkin, "The Future of the Document," *Forbes ASAP* October 9, 1995, 46.

8. From the Paper Federation of Great Britain. See their Web site at <http://www.paper.org.uk/>.

9. In 1995, CAP Ventures estimated that business and office consumption in the United States constituted 32 percent of total paper consumption (*The Future of Paper: Executive Summary*, 6). In the United Kingdom, the proportion of office paper as a function of overall paper consumption is within a similar range. The Paper Federation of Great Britain, for example, combines business communications, professional referencing, and consumer paper (e.g., direct mail) under the term *graphics*. Graphics paper constituted 37 percent of all consumption of paper in 1999.

10. Uncoated groundwood is the paper grade used for newsprint and, outside of office environments, represents a large proportion of the paper market (for newspapers). However, within the office, it is used for poorer-quality office publications. There is a trend toward less of this kind of end use.

11. This comes from an intranet survey reported by CAP Ventures. (*The Future of Paper: Business Communications*, 22).

12. A study carried out by International Data Corp., cited by S. Greengard in "Getting Rid of the Paper Chase," 69.

13. According to research carried out by Xerox PARC's Information Center.

14. "Battle Is on to Control Avalanche of Paper in the Electronic Office," *Financial Times Review,* November 1, 1995.

15. P. Saffo, "The Electronic Piñata." A piñata is a hollow sculpture (often shaped like an animal) featured at Mexican children's parties. The piñata, made of cardboard or papier-mâché, is filled with candy and hung by a rope. Children are blindfolded, spun around several times, and then given a stick to hit it. Onlookers cheer, and when the piñata is finally split open, the candy spills out and all rush to gather the goodies.

16. J. J. Gibson, *The Ecological Approach to Visual Perception,* 40.

17. Don Norman has written about this issue in many different books and articles, but for the most comprehensive coverage, see *The Design of Everyday Things.* See also Bill Gaver's work on this topic, for example, W. W. Gaver, "Technology Affordances."

18. Most notably Marge Eldridge, Kenton O'Hara, William Newman, Dave Randall, Mark Rouncefield, Alex Taylor, and Phil Tyson.

Chapter 2

1. This is from a study carried out by the International Data Corporation, cited by S. Greengard in "Getting Rid of the Paper Chase."

2. As cited in *Seybold Seminars Online,* San Francisco, September 5, 1996.

3. *San Francisco Business Times,* October 20, 1997.

4. According to a survey by Deloitte and Touche in the early 1990s, as reported in "The Office of the Future," 3.

5. As reported by M. Skapinker, "Warm for Forms," 166.

Chapter 3

1. N. Beck, *Shifting Gears.*

2. Though, of course, there are problems here. See the chapter entitled "Home Alone" in John Seely Brown and Paul Duguid's book *The Social Life of Information,* 63–89.

3. For more detail on the inner workings of the IMF, see R. H. R. Harper, *Inside the IMF.*

4. For more detail on the method, see A. J. Sellen and R. H. R. Harper, "Paper as an Analytic Resource for the Design of New Technologies."

5. This also involved two of our colleagues at Xerox, Marge Eldridge and William Newman.

6. The data for only eight of the sixteen knowledge workers are shown. For the other eight economists, it was difficult to obtain a full five-days' worth of data. Some were out of the office because of work commitments and illness. Others were simply too busy to be able to participate on some days. Similarly, for our analysis of administrative staff, results from only five of the seven people in the sample are included.

7. A. Kidd, "The Marks Are on the Knowledge Worker."

8. As we discuss in chapter 5, these observations owe much to the work of Christian Heath and Paul Luff, who have studied collaborative processes in fine detail through analyzing videotaped interactions among co-workers in a variety of different work settings. See, for example, P. Luff, C. Heath, and D. Greatbatch, "Tasks-in-Interaction: Paper and Screen Based Documentation in Collaborative Activity," as well as P. Luff, J. Hindmarsh, and C. Heath, eds., *Workplace Studies*.

9. For a review, see R. A. Hirscheim, *Office Automation*.

10. This study is cited by H. Poppel, "Who Needs the Office of the Future?"

11. Here our categories were more detailed, but we were able to compare by merging several of them. For example, the Booz-Allen, & Hamilton category "Creating Documents" corresponded to a combination of our categories "Drafting Own Text," "Editing Own Data," and "Reviewing Others' Data."

12. R. A. Hirscheim cites this study by Engel et al. (1979) in *Office Automation*.

13. Categories were mainly matched again by merging our own categories. For example, the Engel et al. category "Typing" corresponded to our categories "Typing Text," "Formatting Text," and "Form Filling."

14. For example, Martha Feldman's study of government policy analysts in the United States shows that they devote more or less all of their time to the production, review, and revision of documents. Her study confirms the general fact that knowledge work is document-centered. See M. S. Feldman, *Order without Design*. Other research, such as that of Graham Button and Wes Sharrock, has shown that a large part of the meetings in software engineering work actually involves constituting and orienting toward documents. See G. Button and W. Sharrock, "Problem Solving in the Work of Engineers." Research by John Bowers and James Pycock in office equipment design has also confirmed these findings. See J. Bowers and J. Pycock, "Talking Through Design." It appears, then, that work that centers on documents cuts across a broad range of settings.

15. M. J. Muller et al., "Telephone Operators as Knowledge Workers."

Chapter 4

1. For a good if somewhat dated review of this literature, see A. Dillon "Reading from Paper versus Screens."

2. Full details of this study can be found in A. Adler et al., "A Diary Study of Work-Related Reading."

3. Thanks to Annette Adler for providing this description.

4. For more detail on this study, see K. O'Hara and A. J. Sellen, "A Comparison of Reading On-line and Paper Documents."

5. A final feature of paper that may well be important in navigation is the relation between information and its location on a page. Some of the readers in our laboratory study commented that they could remember the approximate spatial location of a piece of text or a picture within its physical page. This is a well-established phenomenon in the psychological literature (see, for example, E. Rothkopf, "Incidental Memory for Location of Information in Text"). Here the finding is that people reading from paper develop an "incidental memory" of the spatial position of text or pictures during the course of reading. It is incidental because readers are not instructed to remember where things are on the page—this seems to occur as a side effect of the reading.

Why this happens is not entirely clear, but theories have been proposed that readers are developing a visual image of a page as they read, using reference points such as pictures or even the corners of a page as anchors. Thus, there seems to be an advantage, at least from the point of view of developing this visual memory, to presenting information that is fixed to its physical page.

6. See, for example, F. J. DiVesta and S. G. Gray, "Listening and Notetaking," and K. A. Kiewra, "A Review of Note-Taking."

7. This brings to mind some observations made in 1987 by an English teacher, Marcia Halios, who observed that her students who used a Macintosh computer produced consistently worse essays than those who used IBM computers. One theory was that the poorer (in those days) interface offered by the IBM computers made it harder for students to modify and "tweak" what they were writing. As a result, they tended to plan their compositions in advance more than the Macintosh students did, resulting in better, more coherent essays (M. P. Halios, "Student Writing: Can the Machine Maim the Message?").

Chapter 5

1. These findings are based on extensive studies carried out by Richard Harper along with John Hughes, Dan Shapiro, Dave Randall, Wes Sharrock, Bob Anderson, Dik Bentley, Tom Rodden, and Ian Sommerville. See, for example, Harper, Hughes, and Shapiro, "Working in Harmony: An Examination of Computer Technology in Air Traffic Control." For more detail on the problem of replicating paper with electronic displays, see D. Z. Shapiro, J. A. Hughes, D. Randall, and R. Harper, "Visual Re-representation of Data Base Information."

2. S. Ackroyd et al., New Technology and Practical Police Work. See also R. H. R. Harper, "The Computer Game: Detectives, Suspects, and Technology."

3. These observations about the way in which computer technology can radically alter social interaction were first brought to light by Paul Luff, Christian Heath, and colleagues in their studies of consultations between doctors and patients. For more detail, see C. C. Heath, *Body Movement and Speech in Medical Interaction*, and C. C. Heath and P. Luff, "Documents and Professional Practice: 'Bad' Organizational Reasons for 'Good' Medical Records."

4. P. Manning, *Police Work: The Social Organization of Policing*.

5. A document management system is usually a software package that allows documents to be filed, stored, archived, and shared electronically. Document management systems often also have "work flow" capabilities, which means they have features that allow people to automatically route documents to one another for processing, approval, and so on.

6. At the same time, it is probably the case that the way the buyers organized their files may not have been ideal or perfect. Indeed, it is almost certain that these individuals would have been more effective if they had used filing procedures that were benchmarked against best practice. After all, it was likely that some buyers were better able to marshal their files than others and that some had learnt over the years what was usefully kept and what was not. These lessons could be shared. But this is a very different thing from designing files to be shared among a group.

7. Thanks to Jack Whalen for suggesting this useful metaphor.

8. Note the similarities here to the drastic changes that DanTech made, as described in chapter 2.

Chapter 6

1. For more detail, see R. H. R. Harper, K. O'Hara, A. J. Sellen, and D. Duthie, "Toward the Paperless Hospital? A Case Study of Document Use by Anaesthetists."

2. G. Nunberg, "The Place of Books in the Age of Electronic Reproduction," 18.

3. K. O'Hara, A. J. Sellen, and R. Bentley, "Supporting Memory for Spatial Location While Reading from Small Displays."

4. This was a research application called the SonicFinder, developed by Bill Gaver when he was a member of the Human Interface Group at Apple Computer in the late 1980s.

5. A description of Dynomite can be found in L. D. Wilcox, B. N. Schilit, and N. Sawhney, "Dynomite: A Dynamically Organised Ink and Audio Notebook." MATE was developed by Gary Hardock, a summer intern at Xerox PARC.

6. K. O'Hara and A. J. Sellen, "A Comparison of Reading On-line and Paper Documents."

7. J. Seely Brown and P. Duguid, *The Social Life of Information*.

8. A good example is Pierre Wellner and William Newman's research prototype system called the DigitalDesk. See P. Wellner, "DigitalDesk," and W. Newman and P. Wellner, "A Desk Supporting Computer-Based Interaction with Paper Documents."

Chapter 7

1. J. Yates, *Control Through Communication: The Rise of System in American Management.*

2. C. Marvin, *When Old Technologies Were New: Thinking about Electronic Communication in the Late Nineteenth Century.*

3. The most famous was the work of Frederick Taylor. See F. W. Taylor, *The Principles of Scientific Management.*

4. One of the earliest expositions of this was in J. G. March and H. A. Simon, *Organizations,* though it was not until the publication of R. A. Hirscheim, *Office Automation: A Social and Organizational Perspective,* that the implications for technology were considered. Since that time, there has been a great deal of research, including updates by March (e.g., "How Decisions Happen in Organizations"). For a pointer toward the literature, see R. H. R. Harper, *Inside the IMF.*

5. Though it is not possible to list all this research, one of the most comprehensive overviews can be found in P. Luff, J. Hindmarsh, and C. Heath, eds., *Workplace Studies.*

6. Interestingly, though, one tends to find that those designs or features of design that are most successful are those that build on users' preexisting understanding or models of how things work. Similarly, technology that is thrown out into the real world often succeeds or fails depending on how well it fits with people's existing infrastructures. Take the PalmPilot, for example. The fact that the contents of the device could be easily synchronized with the contents of a person's desktop PC is one of the reasons often cited for its success.

7. It's no wonder, then, that Strassman found that knowledge workers typically use 300 percent more paper than the average user does. See P. A. Strassman, *Information Payoff: The Transformation of Work in the Electronic Age,* 167.

8. There are exceptions here. For example, computers are often used (in conjunction with paper) during authoring, which is a crucial part of knowledge work.

References

Ackroyd, S., R. Harper, J. Hughes, D. Shapiro, and K. Soothill. *New Technology and Practical Police Work*. Milton Keynes, U.K.: Open University Press, 1992.

Adler, A., A. Gujar, B. Harrison, K. O'Hara, and A. J. Sellen. "A Diary Study of Work-Related Reading: Design Implications for Digital Reading Devices." In *Proceedings of CHI 98: ACM Conference on Human Factors in Computing Systems*, 241–248. New York: Association for Computing Machinery, 1998.

Beck, N. *Shifting Gears: Thriving in the New Economy*. New York: Harper-Collins, 1992.

Bowers, J., and J. Pycock. "Talking Through Design: Requirements and Resistance in Cooperative Prototyping." In *Proceedings of CHI 94: ACM Conference on Human Factors in Computing Systems*, 299–305. New York: Association for Computing Machinery, 1994.

Bush, V. "As We May Think." *Atlantic Monthly* (July 1945).

Button, G., and W. Sharrock. "Problem Solving in the Work of Engineers." In *Proceedings of Workplace Studies: An International Colloquium on Work, Interaction, and Technology*. King's College, University of London, September 1995, 7–8.

Dillon, A. "Reading from Paper versus Screens: A Critical Review of the Empirical Literature." *Ergonomics* 35, no. 10(1992): 1297–1326.

DiVesta, F. J., and S. G. Gray. "Listening and Notetaking." *Journal of Educational Psychology* 64 (1972): 278–287.

Engel, G., J. Groppuso, R. Lowenstein, and W. Traub. "An Office Communications System." *IBM Systems Journal* 18, no. 3 (1979).

Feldman, M. S. *Order without Design: Information Production and Policy Making*. Palo Alto, Calif.: Stanford University Press, 1989.

The Future of Paper: Business Communications. Norwell, Mass.: CAP Ventures, 1995.

The Future of Paper: Executive Summary. Norwell, Mass.: CAP Ventures, 1995.

Gaver, W. W. "Technology Affordances." In *Proceedings of CHI 91: ACM Conference on Human Factors in Computing Systems.* New York: Association for Computing Machinery, 1991.

Gibson, J. J. *The Ecological Approach to Visual Perception.* New York: Houghton Mifflin, 1979.

Gitelman, L. *Scripts, Grooves, and Writing Machines: Representing Technology in the Edison Era.* Palo Alto, Calif.: Stanford University Press, 1999.

Greengard, S. "Getting Rid of the Paper Chase," *WorkForce* 78, no. 11 (1999).

Halios, M. P. "Student Writing: Can the Machine Maim the Message?" *Academic Computing* (Jan. 1990): 16–19, 45–47.

Hardock, G. "A Marking-Based Text Editing System for Collaborative Writing." Master's thesis. Dept. of Computer Science, University of Toronto, 1993.

Harper, R. H. R. "The Computer Game: Detectives, Suspects, and Technology." *British Journal of Criminology* 31, no. 3(1991): 292–307.

———. *Inside the IMF: An Ethnography of Documents, Technology, and Organizational Action.* London: Academic Press, 1998.

Harper, R. H. R., J. A. Hughes, and D. Z. Shapiro. "Working in Harmony: An Examination of Computer Technology in Air Traffic Control." In *Studies in Computer Supported Cooperative Work: Theory, Practice and Design,* ed. J. M. Bowers and S. D. Benford, 225–234. Amsterdam: Elsevier, 1991.

Harper, R. H. R., K. O'Hara, A. J. Sellen, and D. Duthie. "Toward the Paperless Hospital? A Case Study of Document Use by Anaesthetists." *British Journal of Anaesthesia* 78(1997): 762–867.

Heath, C. C. *Body Movement and Speech in Medical Interaction.* Cambridge: Cambridge University Press, 1986.

Heath, C. C., and P. Luff. "Documents and Professional Practice: 'Bad' Organizational Reasons for 'Good' Medical Records." In *Proceedings of Conference on Computer Supported Cooperative Work,* 354–363. New York: Association for Computing Machinery, 1996.

Hirscheim, R. A. *Office Automation: A Social and Organizational Perspective.* New York: Wiley, 1985.

Kidd, A. "The Marks Are on the Knowledge Worker." In *Proceedings of CHI 94: ACM Conference on Human Factors in Computing Systems,* 186–191. New York: Association for Computing Machinery, 1994.

Kiewra, K. A. "A Review of Note-Taking: The Encoding Storage Paradigm and Beyond." *Educational Psychology Review,* 1 (1989): 147–172.

Licklider, J. C. R. *Libraries of the Future.* Cambridge, Mass.: MIT Press, 1965.

Luff, P., C. Heath, and D. Greatbatch. "Tasks-in-Interaction: Paper and Screen Based Documentation in Collaborative Activity." In *Proceedings of Conference on Computer Supported Cooperative Work,* 163–170. New York: Association for Computing Machinery, 1992.

Luff, P., J. Hindmarsh, and C. Heath, eds. *Workplace Studies*. Cambridge: Cambridge University Press, 2000.

Manning, P. *Police Work: The Social Organization of Policing*. Cambridge, Mass.: MIT Press, 1977.

March, J. G. "How Decisions Happen in Organizations." *Human-Computer Interaction* 6 (1991): 95–117.

March, J. G., and H. A. Simon. *Organizations*. New York: Wiley, 1958.

Marvin, C. *When Old Technologies Were New: Thinking about Electronic Communication in the Late Nineteenth Century*. Oxford: Oxford University Press, 1988.

Muller, M. J., R. Carr, C. Ashworth, B. Diekmann, C. Wharton, C. Eickstaedt, and J. Clonts. "Telephone Operators as Knowledge Workers: Consultants Who Meet Customer Needs." In *Proceedings of CHI 95: ACM Conference on Human Factors in Computing Systems*, 130–137. New York: Association for Computing Machinery, 1995.

Newman, W., and P. Wellner. "A Desk Supporting Computer-Based Interaction with Paper Documents." In *Proceedings of CHI 92: ACM Conference on Human Factors in Computing Systems*, 587–592. New York: Association for Computing Machinery, 1992.

Norman, D. A. *The Design of Everyday Things*. New York: Doubleday, 1990. Originally published as *The Psychology of Everyday Things*. New York: Basic Books, 1988.

———. *The Invisible Computer*. Cambridge, Mass.: MIT Press, 1998.

Nunberg, G. "The Place of Books in the Age of Electronic Reproduction." *Representations* 42 (1993): 13–37.

"The Office of the Future." Executive Briefing. *Business Week,* June 30, 1975, 48–80.

O'Hara, K., and A. J. Sellen. "A Comparison of Reading On-line and Paper Documents." In *Proceedings of CHI 97: ACM Conference on Human Factors in Computing Systems*, 335–342. New York: Association for Computing Machinery, 1997.

O'Hara, K., A. J. Sellen, and R. Bentley. "Supporting Memory for Spatial Location While Reading from Small Displays." In *Proceedings of CHI 99: ACM Conference on Human Factors in Computing Systems*. New York: Association for Computing Machinery, 1999.

Poppel, H. "Who Needs the Office of the Future?" *Harvard Business Review* (Nov./Dec. 1982).

Rothkopf, E. Z. "Incidental Memory for Location of Information in Text." *Journal of Verbal Learning and Verbal Behavior* 10(1971): 608–613.

Saffo, P. "The Electronic Piñata: A Paperless Future Is Waiting in the Wings." In *Institute for the Future's 1993 Ten Year Forecast*, 171–175. Menlo Park, Calif.: Institute for the Future, 1993.

Sahay, S. *The Office of the Future: Technologies and Trends Affecting Paper Use in the United States.* SRI International Report D95–1892. Menlo Park, Calif.: SRI, 1995.

Schilit, B. N., Price, M. N., Golovchinsky, G., Tanaka, K., and Marshall, C. C. "As We May Read: The Reading Appliance Revolution." *Computer* 32, no. 1 (1999): 65–73.

Seely Brown, J., and P. Duguid. *The Social Life of Information.* Boston, Mass.: Harvard Business School Press, 2000.

Sellen, A. J., and R. H. R. Harper. "Paper as an Analytic Resource for the Design of New Technologies." In *Proceedings of CHI 97: ACM Conference on Human Factors in Computing Systems,* 319–326. New York: Association for Computing Machinery, 1997.

Shapiro, D. Z., J. A. Hughes, D. Randall, and R. Harper. "Visual Re-representation of Data Base Information: The Flight Data Strip in Air Traffic Control." In *Cognitive Aspects of Visual Language and Visual Interfaces,* ed. M. J. Tauber, D. E. Mahling, and F. Arefi, 349–376. New York: Elsevier, 1994.

Skapinker, M. "Warm for Forms." *Byte* (April 1991).

Smith, D. K., and R. C. Alexander. *Fumbling the Future: How Xerox Invented, Then Ignored, The First Personal Computer.* New York: Morrow, 1988.

Stefik, M. *Internet Dreams: Archetypes, Myths and Metaphors.* Cambridge, Mass.: MIT Press, 1997.

Strassman, P. A. *Information Payoff: The Transformation of Work in the Electronic Age.* New Canaan, Conn.: Information Economics Press, 1985.

Taylor, F. W. *The Principles of Scientific Management.* New York: Harper, 1911.

Wellner, P. "DigitalDesk." *Communications of the ACM* 36, no. 7 (1993): 88–97.

Wilcox, L. D., B. N. Schilit, and N. Sawhney. "Dynomite: A Dynamically Organised Ink and Audio Notebook." In *Proceedings of CHI 97: ACM Conference on Human Factors in Computing Systems,* 186–193. New York: Association for Computing Machinery, 1997.

Yates, J. *Control Through Communication: The Rise of System in American Management.* Baltimore: Johns Hopkins University Press, 1989.

Index

Page numbers appearing in *italics* indicate illustrations.